Commitment, Service and Betrayal

By Brenda Frazier

Motivational Writer Journey

Copyright © 2018 by Brenda Frazier

Commitment, Service and Betrayal

Printed in the United States of America

ISBN 978-0-9990755-6-2

All rights are reserved solely by the author. The author declares that the contents are original and do not infringe on the rights of any other person.

No part of this book may be reproduced in any form except with permission from the author. The views in this book are not necessarily the views of the publisher.

Dedication

To the Love of My Life, Tommy Lee Frazier. God ALWAYS knew what I needed before I asked. Being so elated, God answered what I asked for and granted it all in you when I needed you most. To my mother, Viola Mae Legree-Toomer, whose heavenly-bound spirit will live in this life of mine forever. I would be so remised if I did not mention our children, Timmy (Rae), Troy (Lauren), Adam (Denise), Megan, Trevino, Harper and Dylan for their love and support.

Preface

Today is the day that I will start this book on the Life of Brenda Gale Toomer-Frazier. In this world, some of us serve a God (Christianity) that we do not know who He looks like. Although others have chosen to discriminate based on sex, origin, creed and beliefs, we are all created in the image of God. What if God is in the form of a woman with male and female attributes and is comprised of many colors? We would be very surprised at the end of our lives to discover that our life was lived in iniquity because of ignorance.

Based on this learned behavioral trait called racism and discrimination, I regretfully write this book to chronicle my life and court case against the City of Columbia Police Department in Columbia, South Carolina in the Fourth Circuit Court of Appeals: Racial Discrimination case, 16-2096. During the case proceedings, I learned of this terminology of "bait and switch." This is a system that was used in the 1940s through the 1960's, where people of color were hired under a specific platform or criteria. When hired, the criteria are changed in order to discredit the candidate which will lead to these caveats such as resignation, demotion, transfer or termination. In my case, I was offered a transfer to another department but was eventually told that if I did not resign, I would be fired.

This is where the story begins because this is one of the many events in my life that I had to decide that giving up was not the option, yet again. Having been raised in a home of domestic violence, I had to choose the high road. What I mean by the high road is to take on the fact that I was born into this situation. This situation was totally out of my control. My best option was always choosing to move on in the most positive manner; this is what I refer to as the high road. I do believe that life is not what happens but how you choose to react. This is a statement from Pareto's 80-20 rule, "Life is not the 20% that happens to you, but it is the 80% of the reaction to the situation." So, this story is my 80% reaction to what took place on my path to destiny. Part of my life's mission is to keep moving in a positive direction and continuing to uplift and encourage myself and the people who feel that their dreams have been crushed by the evil spirits of the world. In this world, I often wonder what has happened to gaining success while maintaining character, integrity and credibility.

Throughout this life that I have been given, I have been astonished to learn that, "There is no honor among thieves and it seems to be the mantra for people of low morale fortitude." For those who keep looking the other way and keep giving people the benefit of the doubt will continue to get burned as they learn to do better, or they can choose to just to give up. As we are going through, we must remember that these stumbling blocks are designed to set us up for God to lift us to higher heights. This will be the time that God will use these obstacles to make your enemy (wrongdoers) as your footstool. In these times it is key to not to give up and to keep the hope and faith through God.

In the age of the #METOO phenomenon, the systemic problem of sexism and sexual harassment in the era of 2000-2018 is the tip of the iceberg that people of color have been dealing with for decades. For all women who have worked in a male dominant field, experiencing some form of sexual harassment is expected. As for me, I have not been physically exposed to it but I have been approached and spoken to in a manner that was different from my male counterparts. While in conversations with friends and acquaintances, this is a question that is always asked: where do we go from here? One thing I know for sure is that giving up, is not an option!

Through the grace and mercy of God, I have learned to lean not on my own understanding but the vision and knowledge of a greater power in my life. God has sent many angels in the spirit of my mother to cover my life so that the adversary and perils of life will not crush my destiny. Looking back over my life, I can see the safety net that God has placed under situations that has allowed the enemy to become the footstool for the elevation to the next level. This is a phrase from Rev. Gregory B. Cunningham, Pastor of Progressive Believers Baptist Church in Columbia, South Carolina, "Every Member is a Believer, Every Believer is a Witness for Jesus Christ. Go and Tell Your Story." Over the past several years, he has expressed that I have a story to tell. Throughout life, I have told my story on a personal level but in this book will be the first platform of telling my personal story. The plan is to tell this story, but the greater mission is to encourage and promote the theme, "Giving Up, Is Not the Option". To everyone, maintain your faith and hope in the higher power (God). For God will make the path that is ordered for your journey.

Table of Contents

I.	Growing up in Rural South Carolina	9
II.	Domestic Violence	13
III.	College Years – South Carolina State University	20
IV.	First Job – First Chemist In the 1980's	23
V.	Married/Divorced Life	27
VI.	Downsizing – Getting More Courage	35
VII.	Belief of Better Days – Chemist Career	41
VIII.	Chemist – Law Enforcement Officer	47
IX.	Backstabbing, Retaliation and Pain	61
X.	Resignation and Seeking Justice	128
XI.	Keeping It Moving Forward	167

Growing Up in a Rural Southern Town In South Carolina

My first remembrance of life was when I was 3 years old. The only means of knowing that I was 3 years old was by telling this story to my mother. The rural town, Bamberg, South Carolina was an agricultural community where life was around farming and religious living. At that time, my father was a farmer but always maintained some type of steady employment outside of the home. We always had livestock of some sort including pigs, cows and horses. I can remember a particular instance when it was raining and one of the hogs was trying to climb up the steps on the porch. Being 3 years of age, from my vantage point this was like a dinosaur coming up the steps of the porch while I was standing at the screen door. Just as I was starting to scream and cry, my mother scared the hog away and went back to the yard. This is the beginning of my first horrific memory.

My family was comprised of my parents, Ralph Marion and Viola Mae Legree Toomer and five children. I was the child in the middle of two older sisters and brother at the end. In the earlier years, we were a normal family for as much as I could perceive it to be that way. My sibling and I attend the segregated school system in rural Bamberg, South Carolina where life was good. Being the middle child, I was never the one to experience life's challenges first. I always followed and learned from my older sisters therefore I did not have to talk very much to anyone. Believe it or not, I was very quiet. But as life began to become more realistic, my quiet nature had to change. Learning to speak out during times of oppression is not easy but my outbursts only arose during the times of fight or flight.

As a child, I was raised in a home of strong discipline where children are seen and not heard. Out of my siblings, in the occasional instance, I was the one who was most vocal and would speak out in a fight or flight situation. Even though this would be the occasional case, I had learned to respect authority and other adults. My parents did not require us to use Mrs. and Mr. when we would address older adults, although this was the expectations in the southern culture especially when African Americans were addressing Caucasians.

In the early 1970s, the rural school system status had changed from being segregated to integrated. At this time, I was entering 5th grade. Initially I was happy and relieved. There was a teacher who taught my older sister who would make all left-handed students write with their right hand. All summer my siblings would tease me on how she was going to make me write with my right hand. Knowing that I had a stubborn nature, I knew that I would have to succumb to this teacher's demand to write with my right hand.

Commitment, Service and Betrayal

On the first day of school, it was overwhelming to see students that looked so different, but we were all children trying to maneuver through this system of change. Shortly after this shock, I became very elated to know that this strict teacher who instills great fear in her students made the decision to retire. I learned that due to the integration of the school system, many African-American teachers had retired for one reason or another.

Until this time in history, I never experienced racial discrimination. My mother's philosophy was to make sure that her children would know and be aware of the struggles in the African-American culture but up to this point I had not experienced these struggles up close and personal. I had known of Dr. Martin Luther King, John F. Kennedy and Malcom X and their contributions to the people of color during the 1950s, 1960s and 1970s. I can remember watching the funeral of Dr. Martin Luther King on television as well as the booklets of his life and the picture with a mirror and lights on the wall in the living room.

My first experience with racial discrimination had come with the underlying phenomenon of being together but still separated. In my classroom all the African-American students would sit on one side of the class and the Caucasian students would sit on the other side of the room. My homeroom teacher was so nice and did not make a distinction between black or white students. My reading teacher was the mother of my homeroom teacher. She said that all of the African-American students could not read so all of us were receiving the grade of "F". The most puzzling part of this is that I was excelling in all of my other classes especially in my homeroom class where my teacher taught English, Spelling and Penmanship; which is a subject that is no longer taught in the school systems since 2010.

This next incident may not be direct racial discrimination but a step-down version of the root cause. In the rural community of South Carolina, I had an Indian teacher who dressed in her native attire as well as expressing the Sikh culture. In her class, I was taking a test and at the end of the test she made the decision that was shocking. She took my test along with another Caucasian student and made the decision that the two of us needed to retake the test. To my amazement, she did not want to accuse the Caucasian student of cheating, so she asked that the two of us retake the test under her close observation. The astonishing fact was that I knew the material and was not cheating and was not aware that the Caucasian student was trying to copy from my test paper.

In essence she did not want to accuse the Caucasian student but chose to falsely accuse me. For the student it would have been better for her to do the right thing as a teacher and that was to simply call out the student who was cheating. It left me being silently hurt and falsely accused of something that I did not do. As for my father who was very vocal, this would not be a repeat offense. He challenged the reading teacher and by the end of that school year, this teacher retired.

Throughout the remainder of my school years in rural South Carolina, there were many incidences of racial discrimination that were borderline covert in nature.

Domestic Violence

Growing up in a household where there were times of so much great joy and family gatherings, it was so shocking why and when it would all end. My paternal grandparents passed away when I was very young, so I never knew them. My paternal grandmother died when I was a few weeks old. It is unfortunate that I never knew her because I am told that I look, walk and talk like her. My paternal grandparents died a few months apart and at very young ages. This is a stark comparison to men and women today who are living to 80 and 85, respectively. While seeing other friends and classmates with both paternal and maternal grandparents was somewhat different but not overwhelming because I had the love from both of mine.

My maternal grandmother was a soft-spoken woman just as my mother, until they were placed in fight or flight mode. Being the pillar of the community, my grandfather raised seven children (three girls and four boys) and he had a great impact on the type of woman that I would become. As for my father, he was a very intelligent and knowledgeable man but did not have the emotional, spiritual and philosophical mindset to raise a family of four girls and a son. I learned how a man should treat a woman from my grandfather. He taught me that men pursue women and women do not pursue men. He would quote from the bible stating that "He who finds a woman..." It does not state that a woman finds a man. So basically, a woman should let the man pursue her. A man should not ask a woman for money because a man can always find various means to make money but a woman (especially with children) does not have as many resources as a man to make money.

In the early years, family life was just as a young child should expect to be normal. While in a childlike world, there were instances where things did not make any sense. Our family moved from one small town to another small town named Bamberg which was very close to my grandparent's home. This was the first time that I can remember my father being away from us as well as the first time as a patient in a mental institution. Over the next couple of years this would happen a few more times until there were no more options. In this rural southern community, the type of employment would be in textile and/or machinery type of industries.

My mother worked in the textile industry and my father worked in the machinery (tool manufacturing) industry. In the 1960s and 1970s, this community did take on the racial division of the south where African-American were to remain in their respective places. I am sure that the stresses of life in supporting a family while trying to maintain a balance between finances and emotional stability were not easy. Over the years, my parents continued in the process of balancing life's expectations of raising five children and working (scratching out a normal life) in this small southern town. Within the next couple of years, my parents were able to build a brick home on 18 acres of land therefore giving the family a deep sense of security. At this time, my father made the decision to become a farmer while maintaining a fulltime job outside of the home. This was the work ethic that was taken on by grandfather as well as my father. They would take on employment at night which will allow them to farm during daylight hours.

For a man with strong mental stability, this type of work ethic can be attainable, but I wondered if this would work for my father. On the farm, there were 20 to 30 hogs, at least one cow and acres of garden vegetables from cucumbers, tomatoes, field peas, corn, okra and watermelon. There would be 1 to 2 acres of cucumbers, corn and watermelons. I would call this the glory time because life was good.

As children we were expected to pick cucumbers and garden vegetables. Since there were four girls and one boy, the girls were not expected to harvest the corn and watermelon. This type of work was too manly, so my father would hire his older nephews to work the fields. As girls, we would be expected to help my mother with hoeing and clearing the fields. This was a very tedious task and required a lot of patience to follow the direction of your mother while learning to do this task as a young child.

This was the beginning of one of many mental episodes from my father during times when he was angry with mother and/or the stresses of life. It often rained or looked like it was about to rain in the south, but it didn't. That was just how weather patterns were. We called it, "calling for rain." During times when it does rain, thunder and lightning comes along with the rain or there are times when we would just have thunder, lightning and wind. On this particular hot summer day, my father wanted to clear the field next to the house, but the weather looked somewhat unpredictable.

My father would drive the truck out in the field so the stumps (shrubbery and tree roots) could be picked up and thrown into the back of the truck. His expectations were of us (the children) to throw the stumps into the back of truck while he drove the truck. Shortly after starting, it began to rain and next, here comes the rain, thunder, lightning and wind. To my mother's surprise, he would not let us stop. He wanted us to continue while he drove the truck. Being the assertive, stubborn child, I proceeded to run to the house because I was deathly afraid of this type of weather. Well, all of my siblings followed by running as swiftly as they could. Of course, my father was angry, but my mother would shield us from his anger.

To our surprise, we learned during their arguments that our father was angry with her while taking his frustration out on us. This is a characteristic of most men who use the children as pawns in domestic violent altercations. This disagreement would escalate to the point where my father would force my mother at gunpoint to leave. It would always happen in the middle of the night while my father would be holding a rifle and sitting in the den. While scrambling in the night to our rooms, my mother would wake us up to get dressed as fast as we could to leave for

Commitment, Service and Betrayal

our grandparents' home just a few miles away. During these mental breakdowns, he would be admitted to a mental institution at least seventy-five miles away from home. During his stay in the hospital, my mother would load all of us in the car, we would travel every week to visit him until he came home again.

Over the next several years, this would happen a few more times but only one time I remember my father hitting my mother, but I am sure there were other times behind closed doors. Just as I feel that giving up is not an option, when an individual has had enough, there will be no turning back. Well, my mother was at this point of having had enough. She and my entire family were grieving the loss of her mother, our grandmother. During the last argument, this time instead of my mother leaving at gunpoint, my father was forced to leave at gunpoint. It would have been the best situation if he had returned to the hospital for mental treatment.

This time this did not happen. Unfortunately, over the next couple of weeks (which seemed like a few days), my father would return to torment us while my mother was at work. Once he had returned to look through the house for guns. On his last return, he and my mother were arguing which eventually turned into physical fighting while both of them are tussling for the gun. This led my siblings and I to get involved to help our mother. At this time, my brother ran outside and hid in the yard and my younger sister ran to our bedroom.

My siblings and I were able to push my father onto the stoop. In the meantime, my mother was able to get the gun away from him. He ran to his vehicle to get another gun. At this time, he broke the window in the door, we ran to my mother's room and my mother was on the opposite side of the door. My father began shooting through the door then my younger sister was coming up the hallway and was shot in the chest.

My father shot several bullets but only one hit my sister while the others hit the closet door at the end of the hall. I screamed and ran to her rescue while she was lying on the floor. Before the altercation began, my mother was able to call my aunt and uncle, who lived a few miles away near my grandparents' home. They arrived just as the shooting had stopped and my aunt was able to get my father to leave so that they could get into the house. Just as law enforcement arrived, my uncle was able to get into the house.

My mother had a broken nose from the fight and my sister was shot. Although my mother was able to heal from the broken nose, my sister died. In a rural community, we were now known as the children of the father that committed murder and was sent to prison for manslaughter. As children, we were now scared for the rest of our lives in this rural community. This left my mother with the task of trying to put all of the shattered pieces of her's and our lives back together again. It is ironic that this is being written during the time of the shooting at Marjory Stoneman Douglas High School in Parkland, Florida which brought on the call for federal assault gun regulation. Our president and legislators are under the impression that if all parties (good and evil) have guns then the evil may not take lives or at least not as many lives. Well, for this situation, both of my parents had a gun, but we lost my sister.

While being in my teenage years and under the stigma of peer pressure, I became more of an introvert. I did not seek out acquaintances and did not have a desire to seek new friendships. The only people that I would talk to were relatives and friends of my siblings. Looking back, this was my coping mechanism. To keep from being hurt, I chose not to trust anyone to alleviate the possibility of rejection.

College Years – First Chemist Job

Graduation from high school in 1978 was an opportunity to start a new beginning. Over the past several years, I did not have control over the situations that happen but now I have total control so at least that was what I was thinking. Due to the financial situation at home, I was not able to start college in the fall of the 1978 but took a job as sales clerk at Big K Edwards the first chain store in the making of Walmart. At that time, my two older sisters were already in college and my mother was so overwhelmed with all of the girls leaving for school that I made the decision to not go but to wait until the beginning of the next year.

Upon entering school in 1979 at South Carolina State College, I moved into Bradham Hall that seemed to be miles away from the rural small town that I grew up in but it was not. All of the students were just like me. They also grew up in small rural towns across the state of South Carolina. Making a decision on what my major will be as a student was not very difficult because I always wanted to own my own business. After much research and evaluation of the student handbook, I chose to major in business administration. This was my thought process of choosing a major that would play a major role in determining my destiny. Plans were to graduate with a degree in business administration so that I could own a business. I was not sure of the type of business, but this would develop over the next four years.

After registering for classes, I learned the difference between high school and college instructors. In high school, teachers were preparing us for colleges whereas the college teachers were preparing us for life. While attending a Historically Black College and University (HBCU), the focus being taught was to build skill sets that will help the student navigate the world's obstacles. It would have been a luxury to be in a world that saw the contributions of our education instead of the color of our skin and culture.

Once choosing my classes such as Math 101, English 101, Earth Science, ROTC and Economics, I was ready to move forward, so I thought. All the professors were just as I had imagined them to be except for the Earth Science Professor. As I had observed, at least 90% of the instructors in the science departments were from foreign countries. The language barrier was somewhat of a challenge in learning the material. Sitting in the front of any room is a principle I learned as a child. In church, I always would sit on the second row per my mother's instructions. While in school, this principle had never been forgotten. In class this approach was utilized but while sitting on the first row and/or the front of the classroom, I was not sure that this was helping. With time and patience, I was able to meet this challenge. The Earth Science instructor was very difficult to understand but not the material. His class size was overwhelming for him and not to my liking as well. This is the tactic that he used to make students drop out by having them to stand to answer questions that was basic knowledge about the earth.

To my surprise, students could not answer these questions. This was the question that he asked each student and if they could not answer this question, he suggested that they should drop out this class because they would be within the timeframe to drop the class without penalty. This was the question, "Based on this information, if a person weighs 160 pounds on earth and 20 pounds on the moon, what statement could be determined from this information?" I was seated on the last row in the third seat by the window. The instructor started asking students that were seated next to the door.

No one could answer the question correctly until he asked me. I said that based on the statement, "On the moon, a person would weigh 1/8 of what the person would weigh on earth". The instructor made me come up to the front of the room to repeat the answer. At that time, I was not sure if I had answered the question correctly due to the fact that I may not have understood him due to his Caribbean accent. This class met two times a week so on the next day of class, at least half of the students dropped out of the class.

This instructor was difficult to some but not to me. Believe it or not, I enjoyed being a student in the class. For some strange reason he became my mentor by asking challenging questions. During this semester, these were the challenging questions from him, "Why did I choose business administration as my major?" and "Does my family own a business?" and "If my family does not own a business, I will probably be the business owners' secretary." I passed the class with an "A" and the instructor suggested that I should consider changing my major to Chemistry. He felt that this would better suit the skill sets that I had developed from high school. After returning from the summer break, I changed my major to Chemistry while minoring in mathematics. As they say, the rest of the story was history.

The first 3 years of college had moved along with standard practice of studying and learning to build an outstanding college transcript for future career prospects. One opportunity really stood out between the sophomore and junior years. Being a member of the Beta Kappa Chi Scientific Honor Society allowed the opportunity to participate in Medical Minority Summer Programs for six weeks at the Medical University of South Carolina in Charleston, South Carolina. In this program, I would work with nurses and doctors on the research of sickle thalassemia and sickle cell anemia.

In the 4th year while in the final stretch toward graduation, times were good but stressful. After receiving the Burrell E. Workman scholarship, this allowed the opportunity to obtain a Cooperative Education internship at a local pharmaceutical company as a research technical assistant. The most thrilling moment was having the ability to purchase my first car, a bright red Mazda GLC. This car looked like a red ball of glass on wheels.

Commitment, Service and Betrayal

The Dean of the Natural Science department had approached me about applying for a scholarship from the Environmental Protection Agency. I was grateful that he would considered that I should apply and to know that I had received the scholarship was outstanding. This scholarship made it possible to pay off tuition debt and left enough money to use for a down payment on a new car. Having a car made it possible to take classes and work at the pharmaceutical company. This allowed the ability to complete my degree along with building a career after graduation.

It all came to fruition when I accepted an offer from the Engineering Technical Director to start working in the Research and Development Department after graduation. Once hired, I learned that I was the first women as well as African American to work in the Cooperative Education Program at this company. During the process of obtaining this position, the director and assistant director of the College Cooperative Education Program expressed that they were surprised with this company's acceptance of my employment because they have tried for years to place students but was not successful with their plan.

The first job of my career as a Research Technical Assistant had rendered the opportunity to work with others in the engineering and chemical disciplines. After a few years in this department, I had the opportunity to transfer to the Quality Control Department as a Quality Control Technician. Even though this was a 24 hour/7day position, I was open to the challenge as an young adult with nothing to do but work, so I thought. Prior to changing positions, a young man pursued and asked for my hand

Commitment, Service and Betrayal

in marriage and I accepted. Life was wonderful as we navigated through our years of making a life together.

Next came the shake-up of my career. It would be my installment to the now, "#METOO" campaign against sexual harassment. After about a year into this position, an area manager approached and asked me to have breakfast with him since we were both getting off work in the morning. I was astonished by him asking since we were both married. He was married to my co-worker who worked on another shift. Usually I am getting off while she was beginning her work day. To promote cross training, I would sometimes be on the same shift with her. When he asked, I just laughed and told him that I was going home to my house and not his house for breakfast. At this time, I lived at least 45 miles away from the pharmaceutical company and did not have an interest in him.

He did not take no for my answer. For the next several months, he would call the laboratory trying to get me on the phone. Most of the gentlemen on the shift would take the calls and run interference so that I would not have to speak with him. This man's advances had become a bit too much along with the traveling back and forth to work during various times especially since being newly married. I made the decision to start looking for a career closer to my home.

While still working and a few days after accepting a position at another company, the persistent co-worker who also is an area manager was able to reach me on the phone in the lab. We were very busy this night so the gentlemen that I work with were not able to answer the phone, so I took the call. After he realized it was me, once again he made the same request. This was my response, "You should be ashamed of yourself by making such a request, simply because I work with your wife. I should tell her what you are doing."

Well, this man made the decision to call his wife that morning and tell her that I have been pursuing him. When his wife reported to work, she came to the laboratory and asked me, "What was going on with her husband?." First of all, I was in total shock that this man flipped the story by putting the blame on me. All of the parties were Caucasian except me, so I wondered if they were going to tell the truth or support the area manager's untruths. Before approaching me, the area manager's wife had a conference with the Quality Manager and his assistant. It turns out that this area manager had a long trail of infidelity as well as a reputation of womanizing. Even though this is known about him, this may or may not make his false claim creditable.

On my way to the door, the Quality Manager and his assistant stopped and asked why I did not tell them that this was happening. At this time, the Quality Manager had known that I would be leaving in the next few weeks. Surprisingly, they did not believe the area manager but I was somewhat astonished with his wife's response. She had requested to not work in the laboratory or shift with me. Once again, what did I do? Where do I go from here? Live my life to the fullest and move on to the next level.

Married and Divorced Life

On November 24, 1984, I married the love of my life (so I presumed to be the case) with the plans of having at least four children (two boys and two girls) and growing into old age with this person. Shortly after starting my career with one of the largest papermaking companies in the southeast as an Environmental/Analytical Technician, I was pregnant with my first born, a son. A few years later, I had a daughter. Married life was good and we had a few ups and downs but overall, I thought that we were happy. While working and trying to balance being a mother and wife, it was at times very exhausting, so I made the decision that the two children were enough.

For fifteen years, the life of raising two children and being married was wonderful as though we lived in the white house with the grand picket fences. We lived on about two acres in a large brick house in a rural countryside outside the capital city in South Carolina. Over the years I had the responsibility of looking after my mother who was diagnosed as a diabetic. My two older sisters were not residents of South Carolina, but my brother lived just a few miles away. Over the years, my mother's health was not the best, so I was very appreciative of her helping by coming to live with us during the summers while the children were out of school. This was helpful in two ways; for the children, as well as the ability to see her daily. She was able to spend valuable and precious time with the children.

It was hard to rationalize that my husband had a problem with my mother staying while helping with the children. After all, her presence gave us both peace of mind. This would also give them more bonding time with their grandmother. As time progressed, I came to realize why he had a problem with this situation. Since he worked rotating shifts, on his days off, the children would be in school and I would be away at work, so this would allow him to fish, hunt and play golf. This is what I believed for quite some time until I overheard him tell the children that they will cramp his style when they were out of school and at home with their grandmother. Their father made this statement in a joking manner. Sometime later, I would learn that this was not a joke but a true statement. Just knowing my mother, she is very sensitive and observant of his behavior.

The summers in the south are always repetitive with the high humidity and temperatures as well as thunder and lightning that erupt suddenly. Due to the high heat along with driving an old car, my mother's car transmission no longer allowed her car to go in reverse. This was very disturbing and required an immediate solution. I wanted to purchase a car, but my husband did not want to do this. I really didn't understand the rationalization for this because at this time we had two trucks, a car and a motorcycle. All of our vehicles were in good driving condition, so we talked and discussed allowing my mother to drive one of the vehicles. This was going to be for a short period of time while talking to my siblings for their assistance.

It was New Years' Day when we made the decision to give one of our vehicles to my mother. On the one-hour ride back home, my husband did not say two words to me or the children. Upon arriving home, he moved into the guest room. At this time, I realized that the man that I married was no longer in my life. In all relationships, times such as these will only bring growth or departure. It appears departure was on the horizon. For the next several weeks, I became like a piece of furniture in our home. Since he worked rotating shifts, I would only see him on his off nights as he would go to the guest bedroom over the garage. We also had a garage in the backyard that had a recreation room with a pool table and kitchenette. These would be his choice of venues so as to avoid talking about the problems in our marriage.

A few weeks with this type of living conditions was starting to affect all of us but I was shocked to learn the following. He had called my mother and talked to her as though she was a child. These were his words, "Why do you always ask Brenda for help? You always know that she will do anything to help. You have three other children, why don't you ask them so that they will help instead of her?" Mother told him to come and get the car. She is so nervous driving the car under these circumstances. The day of this conversation she would not answer the phone when I would call her. After several times of calling and leaving messages, she finally answered the phone. During our conversations, she told me what happened. She cried so profusely that I couldn't understand what she was saying.

It took several minutes for her to calm down in order to understand that I was married to a total FOOL!!! This was her conversation, "She prayed to God that I would not have the type of marriage that she had with my father." My husband was living two lives. For the past several months, my husband would only talk to her in my presence and other times, he would treat her like the piece of furniture as he treated me.. The reason why he did not want her to stay for the summer was because he was not faithful, and she had suspected his infidelity.

The most committed rule of our home was that there would be no arguments and/or fights. On the next night, I asked him to meet me on the front stoop or in the backyard so that we discuss what happened between him and my mother. At the end of the conversation, we were even further apart because he asked for a divorce. At this point, I had concurred, but I was not leaving my home.

In the south, seeing snow is very unusual. If the south has snow or sometimes freezing rain, it would happen in the later days of January into February and sometimes in the first of March. On this day, snow was in the forecast. On the way home, there was an accumulation of at least one half to one inch of snow on the ground. My mother called to tell me that she was in the hospital due to a stomach virus. Because of the weather, she did not want me to come to the hospital. She was not alone because her sisters were there but they did not stay the night due to the weather. My mother was more concerned for them than for herself. She did not want them to travel home in this weather at night.

Giving this information to my husband was useless because he maintained a stone-faced attitude for not caring. Being the caring daughter, I did not sleep well that night. The next day was Friday so I called my job and told them I needed time away from work to go see my mother who was in the hospital. After getting the children off to school, I started preparing to go to the hospital that was at least a thirty-minute drive from the house. During the entire morning I was calling the hospital room, but my mother did not answer the phone. After telling my husband about what was happening, he maintained the same stone-heart. As I was prayerfully heading to the hospital, I stopped at Walmart to pick up a few items to make my mother's hospital stay more comfortable. She never intended on being admitted. She was initially hoping that the doctor would have given her a Phenergan shot for the nausea and would allow her to go home.

While leaving Walmart, I was able to reach my mother who then told me to come as quickly as I could. On the drive, I prayed the entire way with no recollection of what I passed. After hurrying out the car into the hospital, I did not bother to get the packages from the car. Asking for my mother's room from the receptionist, onto her room I went. She was seated on the side of bed and looked as though she had not slept at all. She wanted help to take a bath. This is when I noticed the bed pan with its traces of blood where she had thrown up throughout the night. After bathing and getting her comfortable in bed, the doctor came in to explain her condition and the reason for her admission to the hospital. At this time the doctors ordered several tests to determine the extent of her condition. I was told that my mother was in the early stage of stomach cancer. My premonition is that she already knew this but chose not to tell me. While waiting for the technician to arrive, my mother's two sisters came back to check on her.

As we waited, the doctors wanted my mother to drink a solution in preparation for the testing. It was not to my mother's liking so she was having difficulty swallowing this solution. My mother and I were somewhat frustrated with the nurse so I chose to assist her. While trying to swallow the solution, she started throwing up the solution and started going into convulsions. This is when I noticed her eyes rolling back and fixed as in a trance. At this moment, all of the monitors started going off and the nurses started running into the room as they were pushing my aunts and I into the hallway. We all prayed that my mother would be alright while being in a state of total shock.

Within a few minutes, a chaplain from the hospital was heading over to us. Being upset, I verbally abused him and told him that I did not want to talk and hear from him. Refusing to hear and believe that my mother could be gone so suddenly was beyond my comprehension. For the next few hours, my mother was placed in intensive care while we were hoping for a positive outcome but I knew in my heart that she had gone to be with God. Her earthly body could no longer take on the perils of the world. Now she could be an angel in Heaven with God.

Over the next few days, I was working in an out of body capacity. My mother passed away early Saturday morning and her celebration of life was on Tuesday at noon. For these three days, I ate very little and did not sleep at all so it was very understandable for the loss of at least ten pounds of weight. I was happy for the weight loss but not this way with the loss of my mother and the grandmother to my children. Now I have neither a father or mother, but my husband has a mother and father. A loving husband would understand my ways and the loss, but I have come to realize that I did not have a loving husband but a person who truly hates the ground I walk on.

Once getting a grip of what was happening, I told my husband that if we did not seek and work on marriage counseling that our marriage would not survive this crisis. It was his decision to find a marriage counselor. After a few weeks of counseling, the marriage counselor met with us together and individually. At the end of the counseling, she told me that I need to start saying, "I do not know" and "No". Throughout my entire marriage, I have taken on the primary role to ensure the wellbeing of the family. This is not my responsibility but the man of the house. After some discussion, I came to the conclusion that this marriage was over. For the next several months, I started to make plans for the care of our children and myself.

Over a period of several months, I learned how determined this person that I assumed to have my best interests at heart, was trying to physically and emotionally destroy me. He pretended the entire time after my mother's death of wanting to repair the damage; he had already secured an attorney. During our last argument and altercation, I was able to get his notes that he was preparing for his attorney. He was making daily notes of his distorted view of the final events of this marriage. He was trying to use the situation around my sister's death as means to classify me as emotionally disturbed. This is the story that was told to me from my daughter that he had taken them to the mental institution that housed my father and stated to them that I will probably end up in this institution. While visiting my physician, he and his mother contacted the office manager to gain access to my medical records in order to classify me as mentally disturbed. Due to HIPPA laws, the office manager, stated that she could not talk to him unless she had my written consent.

Earlier I mentioned that this man still had his father and mother. His father is a Baptist minister and the office manager is the first cousin to his father. Many times, during our marriage, I told him that based on his mannerisms, "You would think that he grew up in my home and I grew up in his."

Divorce is not where I would have wanted to go but I did not have a choice because my sanity was at stake in this fiasco. This is a reminder of the "War of the Roses" movie with Michael Douglas and Kathleen Turner where they were fighting over their home but ended up killing each other in the end. This was not where I desire to be because this man would always say that he would burn this house down before he would allow another man to live here with me. Over the Labor Day holiday and while he and the children left for a Gatlinburg, Tennessee trip with his parents and siblings, I made plans to find a realtor to look for a home. Instead of just looking for a home, I was able to secure a home and began the process to purchase it. Within a month, I was able to close on a house as well as to serve him with divorce documents. This made it all fine. I was able to keep it moving to have the love, joy and peace that God had for my life and the courage to never give up!

Downsizing... Getting More Courage

Black Monday is what it was called. This was the day, October 19, 1987, when the stock markets across the country (USA and the world) had crashed.

"In finance, Black Monday refers to Monday, October 19, 1987, when stock markets around the world crashed, shedding a huge value in a very short time. The crash began in Hong Kong and spread west to Europe, hitting the United States after other markets had already declined by a significant margin. The Dow Jones Industrial Average fell exactly 508 points to 1,738.74."

Starting this job on this day was not Black Monday for me. It was a new beginning as the next chapter in the story of my life. It was a pretty, sunny and warm day in the fall of this year. Due to all the excitement of starting a new job, I did not realize that on the day before (Sunday), my driver's license had expired. Being very awkward and wanting to make a good impression, I did not want to ask my supervisor for any additional time off, but I did not have a choice. Surprisingly he was very understanding and talked about how a similar situation happened to him.

For the sake of perspective I'm here entering this environment as the first African American female to be hired as an

Analytical/Environmental Technician at one of the largest papermaking companies in the country. Just as the stock market crashed and worked to move on from that horrific day, I would learn to take this opportunity and to keep it moving.

In this new career we were called, "Sewer Cops" that worked as "Mailman". It did not matter what the weather may be outside; rain, sleet, snow and heat would come. The expectations were to deliver data on the environmental system as it would impact the company.

Over the next several years, I worked diligently to make a well-established career while having a husband and now two children. This was not a new company, but it was new to this area in the south, so the culture was very different from the corporate office in the north. The Plant Manager, CEO and the chairman of the board of directors were more hands on with the employees because they wanted to be more than just a name and position. During one of their many visits to the plant, they visited the laboratory where I just happened to be standing at the entrance at the time. They introduced themselves and inquired about my name and position as well as my thoughts about the company and its vision for the employees as well as the department's role. The CEO asked about the quality of our work life (parents with children) which eventually led to questions about a company day care system. Large companies with a vast number of employees which travel a distance from large cities tend to have onsite day care facilities. I was suspect of this conversation because I just happened to bring up the topic with my supervisor and human resources a few weeks ago. I'm sure that was the reason for this

Commitment, Service and Betrayal

discussion. If only I could have been a fly on the wall, I would have loved to hear this conversation between management and human resources.

This was a growing company that offered many opportunities to all who were up to challenge. Ready and willing to take the leap of faith, I was able to press forward. Over the years I would have several managers who seen the potential and therefore offered the opportunity to grow with the company. While working with this particular manager, I would notice that he would always look in my direction during our weekly meetings. This would happen for several weeks until I had conversations with my co-workers to determine if they would notice it as well. A few days later, this manager had stopped in the laboratory and asked if I had a few minutes to speak with him. Of course, since he is the manager, why would I tell him no? He went on to say that he would look at the expressions on my face as a barometer to determine if others understood what he was saying. If he saw a puzzled look on my face, then it meant that others did not understand as well.

With all the family obligations, I was able to progress from an analytical/environmental technician to Chemist for this department as well as in the Quality Control division. As the years passed by, this company was growing while other large papermaking companies where looking for new capital. This company was purchased by the largest papermaking company in the world. With this new growth potential, this would mean that duplication of resources would be eliminated. I was able to miss the first of two downsizing rounds. On the third downsizing event, I made the decision to take the severance package with the plan of advancing my career outside of this industry. Over the past several years with this company, I was able to obtain an MBA in Business Administration/Technology Management. Plans were to use this degree to move into a management role because I did not see this in my future with this company.

Unbeknownst to myself, the management team and my co-workers planned on giving the biggest going away party in the history of the company. Since working for the company for nearly 20 years, I had not heard or attended a going away party such as this. In preparation of my final speech, all night and the next morning, I was not able to determine what to say. While looking over my emails from well-wishers, I was able to gather my thoughts from this poem.

"The road to success is not Straight. The curb in the road called Failure, a loop called Confusion; speed bumps called Friends; red lights called Enemies; caution lights called Family. You will have flats called jobs. But, if you have a spare called Determination; and engine called Perseverance; Insurance called Faith, and a driver called Jesus. You will make it to a place called Success."

By Sulaymon Tadese Faozahny

Over the years, I have realized that success is not where we plan to be but when we look back to see where we have come from. Over the years, I have come a long way from the little girl who grew up on a farm in a small town. Due the situations that I had no control over, I am proud to move past the obstacles of life that have turned into stepping stones for improvement.

On this last day, there were people in attendance I thought never knew I existed. To see the area manager as well as the plant manager in attendance was astonishing. When it was my time to speak, as usual, the nervousness went away to allow the living to be in the moment. After speaking and reciting this poem, I looked across the room; the audience was moved to tears. These were emotions I didn't expect to see. The greatest shock was to see my supervisor show the same emotions.

At the time of this departure, I did not realize that I was the last women in this department to leave the company. At this point, only men were left. All the other women had left for other career opportunities and family obligations.

Belief of Better Days – Chemist Career

Being two years into my divorced life, this was going to be a new start. Being up to the challenge would be the only option as the head of the household while looking for a new place to land. Now it is the time to fly and do what is necessary to make things happen. For the next several months, I would update my resume and interview and interview. Within a few months, I would obtain the opportunity of my career; So, I would think!

Using Kelly Scientific as the reference, I was able to land a position a little further from home than I would have liked but I could see the potential. I decided to take it and see where I would go from here. I started out as Research and Development chemist for a company that produced and sold polymer tubing that was different from any other endeavor in my career. As I had worked for the previous company for 20 years, it all had seemed as though I could make another 20 years with this company. After a few months, I could sense a change in the attitude of the Research and Development staff. A few months later, the Research and Development Technical Manager and the Staff Scientist requested to meet and discuss a new idea of shifting positions for a new plan for the laboratory in order to gain national laboratory certification.

Commitment, Service and Betrayal

In order to gain this certification, a new Quality Control Manager position would be created and filled by the present Corporate Lab Supervisor. This would create an opening for a lab supervisor that they were offering to me. I was under the impression that this would be a great career move along with the assistance from the present supervisor. In fact, this was a great opportunity for both of us.

On a beautiful summer day, my cousins planned a birthday celebration. The weather was living up to its expectation to be a hot summer afternoon. All the family had begun to arrive and gather around the pool. While sitting by the pool, my aunt's son-in-law asked about the status of my position at this new company. Of course, I had given the standard remarks to say that all is going just fine. Afterwards, he tells us about his conversation with the Research and Development Technical Manager. To everyone's surprise this manager made references to his plan of getting me and the present marketing director for himself and Staff Scientist in an unprofessional manner. A few months after I was hired, a new marketing director was hired. Just like me, she was a very attractive African American woman. From this conversation, I recalled a few weeks ago while at lunch, the technical manager had asked about how I was related to my aunt's son-in-law. Not realizing this was the reason for the inquiry because he was making these comments about me without the knowledge of his audience.

Once back at work, I had begun to understand the change in attitude and temperament. Over the next several weeks, I made the decision to seek legal advice on sexual harassment. The

Commitment, Service and Betrayal

attorney's advice was that I was very young and still had a long career ahead so therefore I should not want this type of stigma. Looking back, I have come to realize I did have options but was listening to the wrong advice from someone with their own ulterior motives. This legal advice coupled with the high stress level (unrealistic plan from the R&D expectations) forced my decision to seek employment elsewhere. Before their knowledge of my departure, I was asked to go with the Human Resources Manager to the Equal Opportunity Commission Board for this employee who was eventually fired. This realization confirmed my suspicions for offering the Laboratory Supervisor position.

In my career, I had managers who would know the theory and the manual operations of the lab instruments but not the daily operations so if they had to operate the instruments, the managers would not have the capability. Most manager are expected to know the theory of each instrumental analyses but the manual operations of each instrument are not expected because this is the reason why technicians are hired to handle the daily operations. At this company, it was their expectation, that I should know how to operate each instrument as efficiently as each technician in such a short period of time. Here is another example of bait and switch when the expectation had changed after being hired. If I were a male in this position, the expectation would not be the same especially with their unprofessional expectations.

Once again, giving up is not an option so I left and obtained a position as a chemist with a state operated laboratory. During the job seeking process before officially leaving this company, I had an opportunity for a technical laboratory manager position on the west coast's Northwestern Pacific area. After several phone interviews with the headhunter (Job seeking firm), human resources and technical director, I was flown to the west coast for a face to face interview where I meet with everyone. After spending several days with everyone especially the accounting manager (comptroller), she asked me to attend the chamber of commerce meeting that evening. I assume that it all went well because the next day, they scheduled a meeting with a local realtor to look at potential properties. The home and their values were very different from homes on the east coast. Just as the homes were different so were the people.

Upon returning home, one of my friends asked the question, "How many people did you see that looked like you?" Unfortunately, I only had seen two, but they were not at the potential company. With my daughter, we did research using census information on the small town in the Northern Pacific. If I were to take this position, she would have been going with me. Based on the census information, there were only 13 African Americans in this town. This was her response, "If we to move there, it will now be 15!!!"

With all being said, "Here We Go Again!" In conversation with the headhunter, the salary quote for this position was 75 to 85K. Well for me, the offer was 65K along with the expectation that if I would leave within a year... I would have to pay back all the money that the company would spend on relocation as well as the hiring process expenditures.

With these unreasonable expectations, I made the decision to decline. Surprisingly the human resources manager had thought this to be a great offer and had stated for me to take a day to really think about it (meaning to reconsider their offer) and to call her back the next day. She was also upset that the headhunter had discussed the salary range which was incorrect --- so she said. The headhunter was upset and felt that I should take it even though the salary was only 10K below what he had originally advertised. Well the next day, I told her that I would only accept 75k in order to uproot and move my family to the other side of the US. She had stated that she could not offer this salary because it will upset the other managers. Being perplexed, I asked, "How would they know? I replied, "this information should be confidential!" Here I go again, if I were not African American and a woman, I do believe, there would not have been any questions on receiving the original, advertised salary.

Chemist – Law Enforcement Officer

For the next adventure in this chemist career, I had the opportunity to interview for two positions within a few weeks of each other. The interviews were for chemist positions with the same state agency. Perplexed as I could be on how this could happen since this state agency was using the same human resources department. Precariously it all had worked out to my advantage. While vacationing with my family at the beach, I received the phone call with an offer that I accepted. Within a few weeks I began working at the agency that I thought was the best fit for my skills, knowledge and experience.

Even though this was a wonderful opportunity, I learned a sense of appreciation for the duties, but this was not the place that I wanted to be for the remainder of my career. Since the tasks were mundane and predictive, this had given ample time to search for something else. In retrospect my college professors always said, "College prepares its students for careers not jobs. For a job is for only one task where as a career is for a plethora of ideas, experiences and challenges that will lead to many opportunities." With these thoughts, I would press on to the next endeavor.

Commitment, Service and Betrayal

After working for this state agency, I had an opportunity to apply, interview and was offered a position with a local municipality and law enforcement agency in the state capital. This would again be another interesting interview and hiring process. Being invited and participating in the first interview was of something that I had never seen before. It was a hot summer day in August so needless to say all temperatures were rising. As I ascended the steps to the building, I stated to the officer on the other side of the glass window through a screen the reason for my presence. He asked for my identification (driver's license) that he kept along with a form that I had to fill out.

In the corner of the room, I noticed a seat and proceeded there to fill out the paper work while noticing other people in the room who appear to be formally dressed just like me. A few minutes later, the Human Resources Manager came through the security door and explained the process and that all of us would be interviewing for the chemist position on this day. This was the first step in the process then next would be a background check, credit reporting verification and polygraph testing. If we passed the initial interview, then those individuals would move to the next steps. The board interview had consisted of the lieutenant and sergeant from the criminal investigations unit and the deputy chief of the department.

During the interview, it was obvious that the current chemist was not included in the process, I have met key people and seen the potential work area during previous interview processes. A few weeks later I did hear from the Human Resources Manager on moving to the next step by providing credit report information and the background check. She stated that once this was completed with satisfactory information, I would be contacted. She also noted that only three people were chosen from the panel of interviewees to move on to the next step.

During the initial interview process, there was a chemist from the state law enforcement division, so I was not surprised that this person was selected. A few months later, I received the call from the Human Resources Manager that I was selected to move forward for the polygraph test and to expect a call on the date and time. The polygraph test was scheduled and taken a few weeks later and was successfully passed. Realizing that this was going to be a long, slow process was an understatement based on my past experiences of the interviewing and hiring process. With time I had learned that this was not a conventional or standard process for interviewing and hiring. A few weeks later, the Human Resources Manager called and stated that the candidates where down to two people, me and one other chemist. The two of us would be scheduled for an interview with the county laboratory manager and staff in the next couple of weeks. The interview was set but I still was not allowed to meet the present chemist and/or tour the laboratory. At the interview with the county laboratory personnel, the Human Resources Manager, the other chemist interviewee and myself were present.

Surprisingly, I was under the assumption that the other candidate would have been from the state law enforcement division, but this chemist had worked in the private sector. This interview process was different from the others because they were more knowledgeable on laboratory principles and practices as well as the Human Resources Manager was in the room to observe. After the interview, we were allowed to tour the RCSD laboratory, but I was not allowed to tour CPD's laboratory. Greatly surprised, I learned a few days later that I was chosen for the chemist position. At this time, we discussed the reason why she chose to sit in on the interview. The dynamics of the people were totally different meaning that all the county personnel were Caucasians as well as the other chemist candidate.

She was there to ensure the questions and information was rendered fairly. From the questions and information along with my answers, she expressed that the county laboratory manager had stated that with the State Law Enforcement Training (stated in the chemist's position advertisement), I would be up to speed within six months. This was not the final step. A few days later I had to meet with the chief of the department along with the Human Resources Manager and the Deputy Chief. He asked about my educational and career background as well as if I could shoot a gun. He also looked over to the Human Resources manager and the Deputy Chief and stated to them that he will hold them totally accountable for this situation. This was the questions that I asked myself, "What did this mean?" He asked that I take a PAT Test. This being another question, "What is a PAT Test?" Then, he stated that should I pass the test, then an offer would be extended. Later after getting this position, I learned that this was not standard practice in performing this test prior to employment. Once again, surprisingly, I passed the Physical Agility Test (PAT). Finally, I am thinking that I am going to meet the present chemist and see the laboratory.

Surreptitiously, I only had a meeting with the Deputy Chief where she stated the salary and start date, so I did not see the laboratory neither the present chemist. She stated that I would get to see this on the start date.

Giving a two-week notice for the present position with the state agency, I left for the city municipality while hoping for a new beginning. Astonishingly there were challenges that I could not have even imagined. The first day I meet the sergeant who was on the panel for the board interview along with all of the staff in the crime scene unit as well as the captain, other lieutenants and sergeants from various units on the second floor. A few hours later, I was taken to meet the present chemist and the laboratory. Within a few minutes of the conversation, I could understand the reason for them not allowing a meeting with the present chemist and viewing the laboratory.

The laboratory was very antiquated and small. What I mean by small is that all of the laboratory equipment encompassed all of the counter top space with very little work space. I was not aware that there was a laboratory analyst (retired police officer) who only performed marijuana analyses. His area was just as small with only a few feet of counter top space and a desk. The largest area was the office of the chemist which she had stated was only big enough for her work. With no accommodations in the lab, I was given a desk space on the second floor with the crime scene unit.

Feeling that the best place would be a desk in the laboratory but working from the desk space in crime scene unit made it possible to understand the dynamics of the personnel. Which lead to understanding the thought process (purpose) to fill the chemist position. Over the past several weeks, I worked diligently with the present chemist to meet the expectations of this position. Over the years I have worked in the leadership capacity throughout my career. The basic facets of leadership are:

1. Positional Expectations (Outlined in the Advertisement)
2. Tools and Resources to Perform in Position
3. Rewards for Meeting the Expectations
4. Consequences for Not Meeting Expectations

See the Advertisement for the Chemist Position as well as the underlined requirement.

Term: Regular Full-Time
Pay: $45,223 - $59,790/ANNUAL
Nature of Work:
The purpose of this position is to perform responsible professional and technical work in the chemical analysis of drugs and other substances held as evidence in criminal cases; to assist with other criminal evidence analysis, and to perform related work as required.

Qualifications:
Bachelor's degree in chemistry, or closely related field with six (6) month work experience in developing methods and procedures for the effective and efficient analysis of drugs and other substances confiscated by Police Department officers and held as evidence in criminal cases.

Special Requirements:
Must possess and maintain a valid SC Class "D" Driver's License and have an acceptable driving record. Must have knowledge of personal computer equipment with skill in the use of Microsoft Office preferred, utilizing Outlook, spreadsheet and presentation software programs as well as data entry skills. <u>Must possess and maintain or be able to obtain SLED certification within one (1) year from date of hire or promotion.</u> Preference may be given to applicants who currently possess SLED/Drug Analysis certification. Preference may be given to applicants who are a current Class I Law Enforcement Officer.

For the next several weeks, this environment was so different from any place that I ever worked but this was very understandable. What I mean by understandable is that it is very stressful, demanding with direct impact on the public. Be that as it may, I was up for the challenge because if these people can do this, so can I. Trying to be understanding with the present chemist, a few weeks of working together would prove to be an up and down situation. She made a statement to me, "She could not imagine learning all this Drug Enforcement Information at my age!". What she had noticed that I was meeting the challenges by excelling on all the tests on drug information and instrument application in maintenance and troubleshooting.

During this conversation, we talked about the way that I was hired. Realizing that she was not present during the interview process. She was upset with the Human Resources Manager and the Deputy Chief for not including her in the process. I expressed to her that she should not take it out on me because I am the innocent bystander in this process. Also, I expressed that throughout the process, I would ask to see the present chemist and the laboratory. Wow, we were beginning to come to common ground to work together to meet the expectations (purpose). By the beginning of the next week, the conversation would take the days of old and to be short lived as to turn right back to working in a turbulent environment.

Since working on the second floor, I had the opportunity to speak with the Captain of Criminal Investigations. He explained why I was hired. The present chemist had stated that there was such a vast backlog of analyses. Even though the marijuana analyst was hired a few months ago, she still could not keep up with the workload while still maintaining police duties. He stated for some strange reason in the last several weeks, she does not have a vast backlog anymore that she is now all caught up with the analyses. I told him of our conversation on the hiring process by excluding her, but he stated that they hired me based on her request for assistance. Then I asked, why was she not part of the interview process? He stated that she wanted total control of the selection process. Since she did not, she did not want to be part of the hiring process.

This principle, I learned while working in Federal and State certified laboratories, is all laboratories are required to have Standard Operating Procedures. In the first weeks of working with the present chemist, I inquired about and asked to see the standard operation manual (SOP). Present Chemist had stated that she had developed a manual, but they would not approve the procedures, so she destroyed the manual. She was presently using State Law Enforcement Procedures (SLED) that were dated from 2004. These procedures were at least 7 to 8 years old. In conversation with the Captain, I was given contact information for the only African American Forensic chemist in the state, in hopes, that she would be more helpful.

This was like a breath of fresh air. The African American forensic chemist was from the coastal area of the state. She would be the saving grace by opening doors to persons at SLED, County Forensic Chemist, past chemist with this police department and other forensic chemists in the upstate and the coastal area. Per conversation with her, she was once part of the peer review team until her laboratory was able to hire another chemist therefore alleviating the need to seek assistance outside her laboratory. She also stated the present chemist did have a SOP because that was one of the requirements to become part of the peer review team. The peer review members review and approve each laboratory's standard operating procedures (SOP). After meeting the peer review team, they had also stated that the present chemist did have an SOP because they had copies of it. When I asked if I could have a copy, they were not able to present one. For all certified or non-certified laboratory, it is requirement for good laboratory practices to meet quality control/assurance protocols to have a chemist or team of chemists of similar or greater expertise to examine all cases before final reporting.

Back at the laboratory, the atmosphere was not getting better. By this time, I obtained certification to perform marijuana analyses from the State Law Enforcement Division. Being surprised once again, the gentlemen, who was giving part of the training as well as the facilitator for the test, was one of the chemist candidates when I was hired. He was also eliminated during the background check, polygraph and the credit reporting process. This aspect did become somewhat uncomfortable, but fairness prevailed.... I passed the test.

Upon returning to the laboratory, I could analyze and prepare cases for reporting. For the cases to be ready for peer review, the present chemist would review all marijuana and drug cases before peer reviewing with chemists outside of the department. Making note of this factor, the marijuana analyst (retired police officer) cases were not peer reviewed at all. On this day as well as the straw that breaks the camel's back, she stated that this case's terminology (worksheets and reports) was not written correctly. Being confused, I had shown her a case that was similar and asked what was different.

Since this type of drug case and reporting terminology were similar, she signed off on the first case for peer review but did not want to sign off on this one. Her explanation was that this case was not completely right and she was giving the benefit of the doubt for the first case. Disturbing as this can be, I told her that I will be discussing this with the Crime Scene Sergeant, the manager over the laboratory. This was her reply, "I do not care who the fuck that you talk to." After speaking with him and upset with what just transpired, he compared the two reports and come to the same conclusion. In my presence, he proceeds to the laboratory and asked to understand what happen along with similar questions.

Commitment, Service and Betrayal

She had given him the same reason for not signing off on the case as well as stating that I was not trainable and that she will not train me. At this point, she will not sign off on this case or any other cases. Being strange as it could be… from the world of good management practices… when does a subordinate tells their manager what they are not going to do and still have a job at the end of the day.

Upper management then decides to review all the training material and testing that I performed on the past several months and made the decision to seek training from SLED. I understood this to be the original plan based on the information from the chemist advertisement. Currently, they are stating that SLED does not offer training outside of their division anymore. Major roadblock for me. Using the previous contact with the chemist from the coast, she was able to reach a retired chemist with SLED who is now a department head and instructor for a local college where she teaches forensic science. At this point, there is a need to point out the dynamics of the people who are helpful with this situation…. as all are of African American persuasion. At this time the chief of the department is an African American but there are so many issues within this department where I was overwhelmed daily. At this point the Deputy Chief who hired me was fired due to allegations of the mishandling and poor representation in a missing person's case.

Speaking with the Human Resources Manager, I discussed the situation. Here is the HR manager's response, "I should have recorded the conversation with the present chemist because she will deny that she used profane language." Based on the municipality employee's policy manual, using a recording device without permission is against the policy and grounds to be dismissed. This was bad advice coming from the HR manager as I stated that I feel that they are using me to get rid of her. Having been with this department for a few months, there appears to be no one there that thinks highly of the present chemist except the marijuana analyst. Within the department, comments (rumors) are made that insinuates that their relationship is more than just co-workers.

During the months of observation, I have similar concerns as well as the feeling that she does not want me there in any capacity. It should be noted that the peer review team is all Caucasian and they are not as cohesive as they appear. In the African American and southern community, Caucasians may not like and/or care for each other but when the time present itself to choose sides… they will not be on the side of the African American especially when it is or not in their favor. At this point, the peer review team is not the best of friends with the present chemist, but they will not side and/or help this department to get rid of her. Most definitely not to replace her with me!!!

Now Where Does This Leave Me and The Justice in This System?

Commitment, Service and Betrayal

Stagnation of Justice

When Justice Stagnates Only the Fool Hearted,

Will Contemplate Pursuing Even the Just of Causes,

When Justice Stagnates Only the Brave Will Seek Retribution,

For Sins Committed Against Them and Their Kinsmen

Can Any Gleams of Sovereignty Exist

Where Justice takes a Tea Break

And When Justice Decides to Standstill

Will Any Sanity Prevail?

Can Any Unity Ever Be Restored?

When Justice Stagnates, The Supposed Saviors

Become the Enslaver, Who Then Will Stand Up

To Refuse for the People

When Justice Stagnates, The Law Maker Become Peace Detractors

Creating Laws Meant NOT to Ensure Harmony,

But To Bring Woo to the Masses

When Justice Stagnates, They Will Seek to Devour

Those They Once Vowed to Protect.

Stagnation of Justice, The Eleventh Plague Not Just

A Spiritual Fantasy but a Present Reality.

By Sulaymon Tadese Faozahny

⚖ Commitment, Service and Betrayal

Backstabbing, Retaliation and Pain

Working for this municipality, there were many times that I would ask, where is the justice and the means of following the motto to protect, serve and defend your employees who are the greatest asset of any organization? In my opinion Maya Angelou is the greatest poet to walk the face of this earth but this poem takes on a very different meaning of the journey that I had taken with these individuals.

"People Will Forget What You Said, People Will Forget What You Did, People will Never Forget How You Made Them Feel."

For this organization, I will never forget what was said, done and felt through the three years of time with this place. Having the best of thought of working to the best of your abilities in making this a certifiable laboratory, these thoughts were not cohesive with the management staff. I often thought of this old parable, "These people are trying to get somewhere but where, who knows where, if these people keep following the Crab in the Barrel Syndrome, they will always be in the Bottom of the Barrel !!!"

Since working with the present chemist was not as cohesive as planned by the command staff, the Captain was trying to determine another course of action. Using the Lieutenant (who was promoted to Deputy Chief in 2013) at the time, he invited me to lunch at the Capital City Club restaurant as to be away from headquarters to maintain privacy. He stated that he wanted to find out what was happening in the laboratory from my personal experiences and not from hearsay. He also expressed his difficulties in working with the present chemist and understood and believed what I was telling him about the conditions in the laboratory. For this reason, he had made the decision to work on a plan to obtain training from SLED. At this time, he had known that SLED was not offering training, but he would try to use his contacts and/or level of persuasion to make the training a reality. After trying, he was not able to obtain SLED training, so we moved on the next plan to discuss and obtain forensic drug training from the retired chemist from SLED.

With assistance of the retired and coastal chemist, I was able to obtain certification even though this was not the SLED training that was outlined in the job description. While away for training/certification, the present chemist resigned from the police department to take on another position in the upstate area therefore leaving the challenge of putting together another peer review team, so I thought. The first idea was to use the retired chemist as the peer review partner, but this idea would be short lived. While expressing this idea with the Human Resources Manager, she stated that you know that they (Police Department Management) will not have two African Americans working together in the laboratory. Unbeknownst, I learned that the retired chemist, who performed the forensic training, wanted my position for her own personal reasons. In many conversations

Commitment, Service and Betrayal

with the retired chemist, at this state agency they would not hire African American students from Historically Black Colleges and Universities (HBCU). She had spoken of a situation with one of the chemists, from an HBCU, who was involved in a comprising situation and was eventually fired. She had stated because of this situation there was an unspoken rule to never hire African American candidates from HBCU as well as the courses were not comparable based on their standards and expectations. With all the obstacles that people of color would have to overcome in the work world, why would this person befriend and stab me in the back in a flash of a minute?

Over the next several weeks, I would analyze cases with no idea of who, when or how they were to be peer reviewed for final reporting. The management team (Sergeant, Lieutenant, Captain and Chief) was working with the agencies from the past peer review team that was used by the previous chemist that left a few months ago. By this time, there was a new interim chief who was put in place when the previous chief resigned due to PTSD. This would be the continuation of many staff changes in this year. Per management, they did not want to use the retired chemist for free nor wanted to pay her because the department had never paid for the peer review process and have no plans to start. For several weeks, management tried to setup peer review with the chemist from their neighboring county, but she stated that due to personal and work obligations, she did not have time. Proactively, I reached out to one of the other two chemists in the group who were more pleasant, amicable and somewhat neutral to the situation.

She was more open and had given the invitation to meet with them the following week. Over the next several weeks, I would give them my cases, but they would not give their cases for me to peer review. At first, this was understandable and expected but what was not expected were their comments about the retired chemist who had trained me. They did not like it as well as had questions how the retired chemist had peer reviewed a few of my reports. Based on their standards, they had stated that they would not have approved the cases and do not want to review any more cases that have been signed off by the retired chemist. This was very surprising because this retired chemist worked in the same agency that had trained each of the chemists in the peer review team. As a matter of fact, she was part of the management team for this state agency that performs drug enforcement analyses training for a vast number of forensic chemists statewide.

There were so many management changes that it was mind boggling. The first Captain, who was there when I was hired, resigned when the Deputy Chief, who hired me, was fired due to allegations of mishandling and misrepresentation of a missing person's case. The Captain was replaced with the Lieutenant who was on the interview board when I was hired. The Lieutenant had been promoted to the Captain of Criminal Investigations. While standing near the window of the Evidence Property room, in our conversation, he asked how I was doing and on the progress in the laboratory. We talked about the peer review team and the case backlog. He looked puzzled and asked, "What backlog?" He had stated that the outgoing chemist had stated the she was all caught up and there was not a backlog.

Fortunately, the window to the property room was somewhat open and two of the technicians could hear our conversation. They were shaking their heads as to say that this information was not true.

The Captain's back was to the window so he could not see their gestures, so I asked him to turn around to look at them. When he did turn around, they had proceeded to go into the storage closet where drug analyses cases were kept. They arrived back and placed at least three boxes with at least 20 to 30 cases per box on the counter. Being shocked, this was another example of the stories (lies) that the outgoing chemist had told them. While working at CPD, the technician in the Evidence and Property room were the most supportive. I always had to remind myself that they work and receive their compensation from CPD so this is where their ultimate loyalty would be. For some their loyalty and the truth does walk hand in hand so I am grateful that this was understandable during my time with them.

So many incidents and events occurred over the following years until, I started a daily log of these events, as listed,

1. In June 2012, present chemist had resigned therefore not allowing the opportunity to complete training at this facility. The command staff will state the she had left because we could not work together and label it as personal difficulties. A few weeks after her resignation, an investigator with the department saw and talked with her. From their conversation, she had stated that she had heard that people from the department were calling her a racist. I wondered why she was branded in this manner for this situation as well as possible by others from the past.

Commitment, Service and Betrayal

2. In August 2012, Mock Court and Forensic Science Certification were completed. At the mock trial were solicitors from the 5th Judicial Circuit Solicitors' office and all the command staff from CPD. After successfully completing the mock trial (simulation of an actual drug trial case), the solicitor for the defense had stated that she could not wait to have me to testify on her cases because I had answered their questions as though I had experience with courtroom testimonies.

3. In October 2012, CPD Certification Training, Weapon Qualifications and South Carolina Criminal Justice Academy Legal courses were completed.

4. In November 2012, Sworn in as a Class III officer. Before the certification process had begun, assistant Police Chief had stated to the present Police chief that everyone was there except me. Being astonished again, the assistant police chief did not know who I was, and I had not seen the police chief since I was hired. They did not know who I was until one of the candidates with whom I had participated in weapons training told them that I was there and standing at least one person away from them.

5. In March 2013, I attend GC-MSD Instrument Operations and Theory Training in Atlanta, Georgia.

6. In March 2013, I was informed by Human Resources Manager that I could no longer participate in the Police Officers Retirement System (PORS) because I did not perform at least 1600 hours of actual police work (daily street duties) therefore would be placed into the State Retirement System. I was asked to sign documents for this change and she stated that I did not

have a choice in the matter even if I did not want to sign the paperwork.

7. In March 2013, due to with many issues with one of the chemist who did not want to participate with the peer review team due personal and work concerns, a management decision was made to stop giving CPD's cases to her. This would only last for a few weeks because the group decided by stating that I had to give cases to everyone and could not decide who should receive cases. For the past several months, one of the chemist did allow me the opportunity to review and to sign off with approval or rejection of his cases. Noting that he had shown signs of trying to be fair for the moment. As time goes on, I will learn why he had had a sense of compassion during this ordeal.

8. In September 2013, the Peer Review team had come to a decision that if they did not feel that I was ready by February 2014 to review their cases, I will not be able to participate in the peer review team.

9. In October 2013, this information was taken to CPD management and a decision was made to talk with the management from the neighboring county. We were told that their chemist did not have the authority to make the decision to remove me from the peer review team. At the meeting, the commanding Lieutenant for the neighboring drug laboratory had expressed his concerns with one of the other chemist in the peer team as well as with the outgoing chemist from CPD. He had stated that he did like the other chemist and would not want him working and/or analyzing drugs for their establishment. (Wondering what had brought on this concern!!!) He had also stated of the technical

(work related) conflicts between their chemist and the chemist from CPD. There were several situations where he had to be involved to facilitate the conflicts between the two of them.

Another decision was made to train with this chemist, since she so strongly felt, that the training that was received from the retired chemist was substandard to their actual SLED training. While training with the peer review chemist, she had talked about the situation where one of the other peer review chemist was kicked (this was her terminology) from the team because he had lost their cases. In meaning, he did know where they were. When this happened, the outgoing chemist from CPD was part of this situation. The peer review chemist stated that she was instrumental in getting the chemist (who lost cases) back with the peer review team. Now I could understand why he was more supportive of her ideas and attitudes. This may also explain one of the reasons why the Lieutenant from the neighboring county did not care for him. She also stated that because she was Italian she always like to have her way.

10. In October 2013, plans were to attend re-certification training and weapon qualifications. As for the impact on my position as a Chemist, the laboratory had a backlog of samples from 4 to 5 months. While I am away for training, there would be no one in the laboratory to perform drug analyses therefore the drug analysis backlog would become greater as well as the solicitor's office will not have assistance with cases and/or inquiries about cases. This leads to another concern that I was no longer a member in the PORS (Police Officer Retirement System) so why should I maintain and/or be certified as a police officer to carry a weapon.

⚖ Commitment, Service and Betrayal

11. In October 30, 2013, Human Resources Manager contacted me while at weapon qualification training that the Interim Chief and Captain finally signed the documentation that does not require me to be a Class III officer therefore I would not need to complete the training. At 1:30 pm, I meet with the Captain, Lieutenant and Sergeant to discuss the impact of this decision on the chemist position. I was told by the Captain that my work hours would change to 8:30 am to 5:00 pm with 60 minutes for lunch as well as I would no longer have a take home car. Captain stated that as a civilian, I could not have a take home car but would be allowed to use this vehicle for chemist's travel responsibilities. Per Sergeant, since I am a civilian, I would not be able to work overtime as well as will not be able to receive compensation time.

12. To verify this information, I contacted the Human Resources Manager. She explained that the take home car was given because I was a Class III officer and not because I was a chemist. This is the opposite of what I was originally told that I had received a take home car due to the chemist's responsibilities. She also stated that as a civilian, I would be able to obtain compensation time for overtime hours.

13. On Friday, November 8, 2013, due to the fact of not having a vehicle (that is parked in the parking garage), the car did not crank due to a dead battery. This is the second time that this happened in the past month where I could not attend peer review. A couple of weeks ago (October 18, 2013), I could not attend peer review because the brakes failed in my take home car therefore I had to use one of the CSI unit's SUV. Unfortunately, none of the CSI vehicles would crank due to dead batteries therefore I could not attend peer review. Since this happened, I could not attend peer

review and the peer team would not adjust the time to meet. There have been several times that I had to meet at different times and/or change the location to accommodate them based on their personal and/or work obligations.

14. On Friday, November 15, 2013 at 1:15 pm, I meet with the interim Chief to discuss chemist/laboratory concerns with peer review, Class III, position benefits and management support. Outcome of the discussion is to prepare a proposal for peer review along with a budget of the cost. Interim Chief will address the concerns to return the take home car as well as to have access to a cell phone. To address the change in Class III position due to change in retirement plans, he had wanted a copy of the letter from Human Resources. Interim Chief had apologized several times for the situation that has been going on for the past 2 years. To address the concerns, he will get up with Captain, Lieutenant and Sergeant to address these concerns for better (improved) support.

See the memo below that was sent to Interim Chief:

Hello Interim Chief,

It was a pleasure speaking with you this afternoon to address laboratory support/peer review/Class III concerns. I am sending the memo as a recap of our conversation along with the attached documentation. Outcome of the discussion is to prepare a proposal for peer review along with a budget of the cost. To address the concerns for a take home car as well as to have access to a cell phone. To address the change in Class III position due to change in retirement plans per the attached copy of the letter from Human Resources.

Next week, I will prepare and send the proposal plan for peer review using the following chemists for peer team/resources.

1. *York County Forensic Chemist*
2. *Beaufort County Forensic Chemists*
3. *Richland County Forensic Lab Director/Chemist*
4. *Past Forensic Chemist/Consultant*
5. *Florence County Forensic Chemist*

Upon completion, delivery and review of the proposal, I would have your approval to choose the members to meet the laboratories requirement for 100% peer review.

Due to the situation with the present peer review team along with recertification training/weapon qualification, the case backlog has increased from 3 to 4 months to 5 to 6 months. With a more amicable peer review team, I will work diligently to decrease this backlog. We discussed the possibility of hiring a laboratory technician and/or another chemist, we can look into these aspects based on the future direction of the laboratory.

As for improved laboratory support, you will address this concern with Sergeant, Lieutenant and Captain. During this process Captain has been very supportive but just like you he has not received the proper information to address the laboratory concerns.

Submitted Proposal to Address Potential Changes in the Laboratory

To: Interim Chief

From: Brenda T. Jenkins, Drug Analysis Chemist

Date: November 20, 2013

Subject: Proposal for Peer Review Team

Per our conversation and your directions from meeting on Friday, November 15, 2013, I am submitting this proposal for a peer review team that will promote the objectives listed below:

1. Professional, Trustworthy and Mature Team that will work in the best interest of Columbia Police Department Drug Analysis Laboratory.
2. A team that will share forensic science skills, knowledge and experience to further the technical development of the Columbia Police Department Drug Analysis Laboratory.
3. A team that will work for the fulfillment of the true aspects of a peer review team for technical critique of case work along with coaching, mentoring and training that will help with the growth potential of team members.

Reviewing the prospective plan for a new peer team, I have put together several ideas so that the peer review process will have several means in order to lessen the time for the process. Right now, the peer review process takes about 3 to 2 weeks. With the development of a more diverse team, this will provide more versatility to perform peer review.

Projected Plans are to use the forensic chemist below for peer review and/or resources:

1. *York County Forensic Chemist*
2. *Beaufort County Forensic Chemist, Lab Director/Forensic Chemist and Forensic Chemist, respectively*
3. *Richland County Forensic Lab Director/Chemist*
4. *Past Forensic Chemist/Consultant*
5. *Florence County Forensic Chemist*

Option 1

Past Forensic Chemist/Consultant will require a compensatory fee for her services. Within the last five years, she has contracted with three different agencies in two states. Compensatory rate of $50.00/hour for the onsite orientation and resulting online peer review will be initial cost of services. Additional fees may be meals, mileage, lodging and/or incidental expenses as required for the onsite visit to be calculated according to the rates designated by the US General Services Administration for government employees. Regarding onsite liability and legal requirements, Columbia Police Department may want to consider approaching the legal department and human resources regarding their requirements for onsite contractors.

Initially, Drug Analysis laboratory will be requesting at 1 or 2 days for at least 6 to 8 hours per day for an onsite visit to include mileage and meals.

Option 2

Using the other forensic chemists that are listed above, initially I would like to travel to their laboratories for peer review. This will render the opportunity to review their cases while they are technically reviewing CPD cases. The frequency of peer review will be at least once a week, I will visit the laboratory in York County, Beaufort and Florence Counties, alternately. See the plan below to address cutting down on the travel time but using an electronic system as means to lessen the cost for travel mileage and meals.

Electronic System for Peer Review:

    a. *Update Laboratory Information System for report writing such as software upgrades and/or VISION AIR (RMS) applicability.*

    b. *IT (Secure Drop Box System) to check for a means to develop a separate drive for laboratory reports to allow the peer team members to view and make comments. This will be another means to cut down on travel time as well as to expedite the peer review process. This will lessen the time for the peer review process therefore the turnaround time for cases can drop to 1 to 2 weeks from 3 to 4 weeks.*

    c. *Updated Scanning System with the Adobe Acrobat XI Standard for speedy transfer of data as well as to provide the capabilities to convert documents from (pdf) to (.com) for improved report writing. See the attached quotes for this equipment.*

⚖ **Commitment, Service and Betrayal**

Response from Interim Chief on Saturday, November 23, 2013 by email

Hi Brenda

I'm not sure if I missed it in the emails, but I was going to see if you had a chance to put the proposal together. I want to make sure we are doing what is needed to get you rolling right

thanks

Interim Chief of Police

Columbia Police Department

Response from Interim Chief on Saturday, November 26, 2013 by email

Thanks Brenda

I'm working on this as we speak

I have a meeting set up with Captain and Sergeant. I will be sure to take care of it and get you what is needed to make things work for us

Hope you have a Happy Holidays and we will talk soon

thanks

Interim Chief of Police

The Columbia Police Department

> 15. On Thursday, December 12, 2013, arrival to work, I meet with Sergeant (who called me two times on my

personal cell phone) as well as left two messages on voice mail at work. Content of Discussion:

1. I will not be able to attend the class on Prescription Drug Fraud Response (90-minute class) that will be given by the CPD training center because if I should attend the training this will cause a Class I Certified Officer to be blocked from the class because I will be taking up an available space.
2. CPD will not move forward on the training class from SLED.
3. Enquire about assistance from Richland County Sherriff Dept.
4. Enquire about the DEA training and had want to have the travel requisition information by next week, December 16, 2013.
5. Enquire about the FT-IR class and had want to have the information by the first week of January 2014.
6. Enquire about by discussion with the Interim Chief and had wanted to know why I did not tell him and/or Captain.
7. Per their discussion with the Interim Chief, I will continue with the present peer team. There will be no changes per the Sergeant.

Based on the Sergeant's response, I could extrapolate that he did not like that I had a conversation with the Interim Chief. This was their means to retaliate by not allowing attendance to the Prescription Drug Fraud training as well as to continue using the present peer review team to audit CPD's case files for final reporting.

Commitment, Service and Betrayal

16. On Friday, December 13, 2013, I attend the South Carolina Regional Forensic Laboratory meeting in Beaufort, SC that was hosted by the Beaufort County Forensic Laboratory and Beaufort County Sherriff Department. At this meeting, the opportunity presented itself to meet the first and past forensic chemist for CPD.

17. On Monday, December 16, 2013, I would see the Sergeant to return the keys for the travel vehicle, 1999 Plymouth Dodge, and to inform him of the flex (comp and/or schedule adjustment) hours for traveling to Beaufort, SC. Per his calculations, I have 2.5 hours of flex time that must be used this week. With information, I had informed him that I will use the hours on Friday, December 20, 2013 to leave at 1:30 pm. This conversation would lead to discussion for the two (2) business/training classes that will take place in 2014. He told me that per the policy for non-sworn civilian, I would not be compensated for travel time to and from these classes. I would need to decide in order to attend the classes and/or absorb the travel time as I would not be compensated.

    Later in the day, he would forward the policy to reflect the situation after he gets the information from the Lieutenant. As for using flex time, the time must be approved to be used and to be compensated with a schedule adjustment within the same week that the flex time situation had occurred. Later that day, Sergeant called to inform that the information that he had given was incorrect and I would be given compensation (flex and/or schedule adjustment) for travel to business/training classes but I had to use the time the following week. At this time, I have given to him the travel requisition for the DEA training class.

18. After returning from the holiday in January 2014, I had continued taking cases to the present peer review team but was told that they will not peer review CPD's case files after February 14, 2014. Upon returning to headquarter, this information was given to the management staff.

19. February/March 2014, Lieutenant and Sergeant meet with one of the peer review team members command staff on two (2) occasions to discuss the peer review situation. This information was conveyed to me after the meeting that I had no previous knowledge before it had occurred.

20. On March 7, 2014, the other peer review member had expressed to me that per direction from their command staff that they will not peer review CPD's cases. As it can be seen, the meeting that the Lieutenant and Sergeant had had with the peer review member's management staff, did not make the situation better.

21. March 10 thru March 14, 2014, I would attend DEA Training in Sterling, Virginia. The Lieutenant and Sergeant were under the expectation that I was going to drive this 1999 Dodge Plymouth (per feedback from the Maintenance Shop, this vehicle needed to be redlined and taken off the road). Since the vehicle was assigned for chemist duties, it had been in the shop at least 3 to 4 times a year for various problems with the brakes, shocks and transmission.

At the end of day, I asked the Lieutenant on the status of the rental vehicle for the trip. He had stated that I was going to travel to Virginia in the assigned vehicle. Expressing the status of the vehicle as well as that I had no plans to drive it outside of this state. He stated that he needs to speak with the Captain and will call back in a few minutes. It was the end of the day on Friday where I made plans to leave on Sunday morning to drive to Virginia. The Captain called and asked me to come to us office so that I could receive the gas card and the keys to another vehicle. It appears as though they were waiting to see if I was going to drive this raggedy, assigned vehicle instead of using a rental that I requested a few weeks ago.

While attending the training class, it was quite noticeable as well as expected to be one of two African Americans. The two African Americans were women from the south, South Carolina and Tennessee. Overall, everyone was cordial and professional while exchanging technical practices and information. From several of the attendees, they were shocked to learn that I was the only person working in the laboratory as well as to know while I am away that there was no one to respond to laboratory requests. I had explained to them that this is how this laboratory had function from its beginning. From the class, I was able to network to my vantage point that I reached out on several occasions for information on drug analytical techniques and peer review methodology after leaving the class.

22. On March 17, 2014, performance evaluation meeting with Lieutenant and Sergeant to present and discuss the evaluation. Being upset with the rating (2.73) from the previous year (4.03) based on a scale of 5, I've been told that this was a good rating because the criteria has changed. They expressed that in 2014, all employees' rating had gone down with the changes in

all the criteria. The Lieutenant stated this was a good rating that would provide areas for improvement. *I asked for the rating scale for the evaluation and to date, never received it.* The performance evaluation was signed in disagreement with this evaluation. I issued a written statement to the performance evaluation because I did trust the Lieutenant's explanation as well as I was in disagreement with their assessment.

A follow-up meeting was scheduled with the Captain when this written statement was given to him. He had told me that all employee's rating had gone down from the previous year as well as his rating was less than the previous year (I was supposed to believe this without evidence). At this meeting, I asked for a rating scale that would show these changes in criteria, but I never received a copy. In this meeting, the Captain and I had discussed the peer review situation and was told that there were plans to hire another chemist, so peer review can be done in house. As for drug analysis, I was told to continue with drug analysis and he will work on a solution to peer review the cases.
I also told him that if changes were not made... I had plans to seek employment elsewhere. (I already had reached out to various headhunters and employment agencies and had several interviews in place to leave because I did not have confidence and trust in them).

Written Statement to the Captain on Performance Evaluation 2013:

To: Captain, Criminal Investigation Division

Cc: Lieutenant, Criminal Investigation Division

Cc: Sergeant, Crime Scene–Criminal Investigation Division

From: Brenda T. Frazier, Crime Lab-Drug Chemist

Date: March 26, 2014

Reference: Written Response to 2013 Performance Evaluation

This written statement serves as a response to my Performance Evaluation for Calendar Year 2013. For your convenience, I have referred to include the following to this response:

- *A copy of my 2013 Evaluation*
- *Written communication to the Chain of Command*
    - *Email*
    - *Memos*
- *A timeline of verbal communications to Chain of Command*

Background: I started my employment with Columbia Police Department on December 27, 2011. From the beginning of this working relationship, I have performed in a hostile environment that was not conducive to the environment that was expressed during the interview process and initial acceptance of this position. Every situation regardless of how small, turn into a major problem. I have reached out to you, my superiors on many occasions, and each time no resolutions were provided, and the problems only grew. These problems range from the following:

- *A hostile (unprofessional) working environment*
- *Insufficient Training*
- *Difficulties with Peer Review Group*
- *Insufficient Guidance*
- *Not having the trust of the agency*
- *Not allowed to consult with peers outside of the current Peer Review Group*

Because of the disturbing evaluation comments, that are listed in additional comments which are stated on the performance evaluation, is of great concern. This is where the remainder of this statement will focus.

The Peer Review Group consists of members from the following agencies: Lexington, Orangeburg and Aiken counties. Due to the conditions of my hiring and their perception of Columbia Police Department, the group displayed no interested in working with me from the beginning except for Aiken County. For the past eighteen (18) months, the situation has not improved.

<u>*References to communications to Chain of Command*</u>

Listed below are the sequences of meetings/discussions with Interim Chief, Captain, Lieutenant and Sergeant with my concerns of support as the Drug Analysis Chemist for Columbia Police Department. I have offered suggestions for training as well as other options for peer review teams that want to work with CPD.

<u>*Ongoing Situation on Peer Review:*</u>

From February 1, 2013 until July 2013, CPD drug analysis peer review was performed by Orangeburg and Aiken County due the difference of opinions with Lexington County. Up to this point, Orangeburg County had allowed me to peer review their reports until the ultimatum was made to meet Lexington County's demand. I did not have the choice of who could peer review my reports. Either all would peer review or none of them would peer review reports.

On Friday, August 30, 2013, I discussed with the Captain the concerns with peer review.

Plan (Objective) from this point:

1. *CPD laboratory analyses will be peer reviewed by the other two cooperative chemists.*
2. *Since Retired Chemist/Mentor has started the process for drug analysis for the city and county of Sumter, I will peer review her work and she will review my work.*
3. *For peer review analysis, I will give 50% of my work to the two cooperative chemists and the other 50% to Carlotta Stackhouse.*

On Friday, September 6, 2013, I met with Sergeant on the peer review situation and what will be the next step to discuss it with Lieutenant. On this day, Friday, September 6, 2013, I went over what happen this morning with this case as well as other cases that highlighted my concerns that are listed below:

1. *Professionalism, Respect and Trust*
2. *Uniform Consistency in the feedback/opinion from the team*
3. *Constructive Feedback and Technical Critiques*

4. Timely Feedback to address concerns before analyses and reporting
5. Giving and Receiving Feedback in reference to Court (Legal) Experience and Knowledge

On Wednesday, September 11, 2013, I had met with Sergeant and Lieutenant to discuss concerns with the peer review process. After explaining the situation that happen on Friday, September 6, 2013 as well as going over the above concerns, Lieutenant agrees that this peer review team is not meeting the requirement for the Crime Lab objectives (scientifically and/or judicially) and for him to have a meeting with each peer team member and/or their command staff will not help to alleviate the problems. Upon his request I will continue with this team until he receives directions from CPD command staff for the next course of action.

On Friday, September 20, 2013, after giving cases to the peer review team, I was told on February 2014 and if there is not improvement in my work. The team will not give their cases to me to peer review therefore I should not be on the peer review team after February 1, 2014.

On Friday, September 20, 2013, this information was given to Sergeant and Lieutenant. They had concurred. I had made the decision along with informing them that I will not use them for peer review from this point on and am waiting from them on the next course of action. Lieutenant will get guidance from the command staff and we will proceed from this point.

Suggestion (Options) from this point:

1. Per information from resources, SLED had train the new chemist from Horry County therefore CPD can request for similar training.
2. Beaufort County has offered to provide peer review in the short term as well as training/resource on case jackets.
3. Request for peer review from Florence County and/or new chemist, Horry County for the long term.
4. Chemist-York County can become a training resource as well as offer guidance for peer review.

On Thursday, October 3, 2013, the command staff from one of the other peer review chemist and Columbia Police department had a meeting to discuss peer review concerns. A decision was made for me to train with the neighboring county but only one (1) training session occurred.

On Friday, November 15, 2013, I had meet with Interim Chief to discuss chemist/laboratory concerns with peer review and management support. A proposal was submitted with suggestion and/or recommendation to address laboratory concerns.

On Thursday, December 12, 2013, Sergeant had inquired about my discussion with the Chief and wanted to know why I did not tell him and/or Captain. Per their discussion with the Interim Chief, I will continue with the present peer team.

In January 2014, I had a discussion with Lieutenant again to discuss laboratory concerns with the backlog, peer review and training.

In February/March 2014, per discussion with Lieutenant and Sergeant, a discussion had occurred with Lexington and Aiken counties to obtain information for this performance evaluation. I was not made aware of this meeting prior to it taking place but a request was made to obtain laboratory case files for critique. The only files that were used for the critique was only files that were returned for follow-up concerns. Per discussion with Sergeant, they are working on a plan to have someone audit my knowledge, skills and abilities to analyzed drugs.

<u>*Questions:*</u>

Per the outcome of the audit, will this help to develop a peer review team that wants to work with Columbia Police Department?

If it is my responsibility to make improvements in the laboratory, why is it that I do not have input in the decision-making process?

<u>*Summary*</u>

It is disturbing that my superiors were aware of my issues and the group's disrespect and distrust of me and yet refused to approve one of the various solutions offered. It is even more disheartening that my superiors who mandated that I continue with the group, decided to discuss my performance with this group of people known to have shown me utter disrespect and offered no professional courtesies. This peer review had never met the true concept of a peer review team that works to coach, mentor and train for technical (scientific and/or judicial) development.

Respectfully Submitted, Brenda T. Frazier, Drug Chemist Columbia Police Department

23. List of events April-May-June 2014,

    1. Continuation of Drug Analyses without a peer review team that subsequently lead to 200-plus cases.

    2. Advertise and interview for additional chemist position.

    3. New Chief of the Police Department was hired.

24. On July 11, 2014, GAP Analysis audit by the County lab director. I did not have knowledge of this audit. Once the audit report was received, I was not initially given a copy. It was a week later that I was given a copy to address the critical findings. This was an internal audit for the police department laboratory to make appropriates changes to work toward obtaining ASCLD certification. The County laboratory was a ASCLD certified entity. This audit was to serve as a validation from all the memorandum that the laboratory was operating in a nonstandard mode.

    See the GAP Analysis below as written by RSCD lab director:

    On July 11, 2014, at the request of Captain Dana Oree, I conducted a "gap analysis" of the Columbia Police Department (CPD) Drug Analysis Laboratory, located at 1 Justice Square. This evaluation began at 8:30 am and was concluded at 2:30pm. During that time, I was escorted and assisted by Ms. Brenda Frazier, CPD Drug Chemist. At no time was I left unattended. Ms. Frazier was extremely professional.

She greatly facilitated the evaluation-it would have been impossible to perform it effectively without her assistance.

Please note that at the conclusion of the evaluation, Ms. Frazier was provided with a <u>verbal</u> summary of my observations, recommendations and critical findings (detailed below). Such communication is not only a matter of professional courtesy, it is also routine practice during laboratory assessment.

I have detailed below: a) general observation or recommendations (i.e. actions that should be strongly considered for process improvement, but do not directly impact quality of test results or safety) and b) <u>critical findings</u> (i.e. actions to taken as soon as possible because quality of test results and/or safety is being/will be impacted). For your convenience, I have divided these topics by subject matter, although please be aware that there is overlap. For this evaluation, I chose not to use a proscribed, pre-published inspection checklist as the nature of my evaluation was "less formal" and not associated with preparations for any official accreditation process (i.e. ASCLD/LAB OR FQS assessment).

1) *Safety/Security*
   The Drug Analysis Laboratory was extremely clean and well organized. Ms. Frazier has made very good use of the space that she has been given to conduct testing. She was able to locate everything that I asked for during the evaluation. <u>Critical Finding</u> – the eyewash stations/showers must be checked quarterly for functionality with documentation of the process. Per Ms. Frazier, at one of these stations is currently non-functioning.

Commitment, Service and Betrayal

Critical Finding – *the fire extinguisher must be inspected as soon as possible (annual inspection required). There should be a fire extinguisher in the drug lab, not just the marijuana lab area.*

Critical Finding – *the chemical fume hood in the Marijuana/Crime Scene Laboratory must remain in the "on" position at all times. There is no other ventilation in the lab areas and the existence of toxic organic solvents presents a serious health hazard to personnel.*

Critical Finding – *the organic solvent storage cabinet is not acceptable. It is not rated for such storage and it not grounded. The doors appear to be broken, A spark or other ignition source could cause a catastrophic fire or explosion.*

Critical Finding – *there is an excessive accumulation of both organic solvents and other chemicals (e.g. acids and bases). Example, I counted four, 3.78 L containers of formaldehyde (used in the preparation of chemical tests). This is an excessive amount of this solvent-it is toxic to the liver. At least one container of an acid was observed to have changed color (sign of deterioration). An inventory of all solvents, chemicals, reference materials, etc. should be conducted and an outside vendor should remove excessive quantities of waste. Minimal quantities of these materials should be ordered.*

Critical Finding – *an air quality test should be performed by an outside vendor to ensure that there is sufficient ventilation to address and minimize the potential accumulation of toxic vapors.*

Critical Finding – *the use of "dormitory" style refrigerators/freezers is unacceptable. One of the chemicals, acetaldehyde (used in the chemical analysis of marijuana), is a potential explosive.*

An explosion-proof refrigerator should be purchased to accommodate this compound (as well as other materials used by chemist). This unit would substitute for *both* of the currently used dorm-style refrigerators.

Critical Finding- a key audit should be conducted to identify all individuals who have keys to the laboratory and access to the large bank vault (storage vault). This vault serves as the short term evidence storage unit for case work and also houses the pure crystalline/powder controlled substances (e.g. cocaine, amphetamine, etc.) *There is currently no inventory being performed on these drugs, so there is no way to ascertain when/if inappropriate amounts are being remove/diverted.* These compounds would be evaluated by DEA and DHEC during an audit and so they *must be inventoried on at least an annual basis*. DEA/DHEC permits reflect the former and current chiefs' names, respectively, but should reflect the chemist's name. It is this individual who must answer to DEA/DHEC during an audit and should be responsible for developing/explaining the controlled substance inventory procedures. *Drug Laboratory permits must be separate from any K-9 unit activities.*

2) Procurement
Recommendation- Ms. Frazier indicated that many weeks/months may pass before consumables, chemicals, reference materials, etc. are obtained, once ordered. This timeline is too long and if possible, should be reevaluated for enhanced efficiency.

3) Equipment/Supplies

Critical Finding – distilled water should be traceable and purchased from a scientific source (i.e. VWR, Fisher). It should not be purchased from the grocery store, etc. The Barnstead distilled water system is obsolete and should be discarded. The laboratory does not use sufficient volumes of distilled water to warrant the purchase of a new (and very expensive) distilled water system. Bottled, traceable, distilled water is sufficient.

Critical Finding – a complete inventory of drug reference materials, reagents, solvents, and chemicals should be conducted on a semi-annual basis. I observed the presence of expired and/or possibly deteriorated materials that should have been discarded, but that have used in testing. The current FTIR (Nexus 470, Thermo Fisher) should be replaced as it is essentially not supported by the manufacturer. The current GC/MS (6890/5973, Agilent Technologies) should be replaced as it is nearing the end of its useful life and is no longer supported by the manufacturer.

Critical Finding – the laboratory is not on UPS; battery back-up units of sufficient capacity should be placed on each instrument in order to protect sensitive electronics during power surges and failures.

4) Quality Control/Best Practices

Critical Finding – all refrigerator/freezer temperatures should be monitored with NIST-traceable thermometers on a *daily* basis. (Note that one explosion-proof unit is needed as described above.)

Critical Finding – the temperature of the "bank vault" may be unacceptable for storage of drug *reference materials and physical evidence. I am concerned that the lack of ventilation may be degrading the evidence. Example, one submitted case supposedly contained "a rock like substance" (as described by the officer), but at the time of analysis, was described as a liquid by the drug chemist. An experiment should be conducted as soon as possible to determine whether alternate storage is needed.*

<u>Critical Finding</u> – *the Duquenois Levine Reagent (chemical test for marijuana) was being stored in the chemical fume hood. This reagent must be refrigerator <u>at all times</u> when not in use.*

<u>Critical Finding</u> – *laboratory weights are calibrated each year by the SC Department of Agriculture. This process and the resulting certificate of calibration are not sufficiently robust for forensic applications. The laboratory should contract with another more appropriate vendor for this function (e.g. Troemner).*

<u>Critical Finding</u> – *there appear to be two laboratory balances in use by Ms. Frazier. If the laboratory is engaged in the analyst of PWID and trafficking case work, the current balances are insufficient for these large cases (Ex. A 10 kilo drug case could not be accurately weighed in the current balances). In addition, the annual calibration certificated issued by Mettler Toledo should be traceable. I strongly recommend semi-annual (versus annual) balance calibration by this outside vendor.*

<u>Critical Finding</u> – *I noted several mathematical/other errors on the laboratory worksheet. The worksheet also reflects the use of four balances. That does not appear to be consistent with laboratory practice. Errors and*

inconsistencies should be corrected as soon as possible.

5) Administrative/Technical Review
Twelve laboratory cases files were randomly selected for administrative and technical ("peer review"). Several corrections were made by Ms. Frazier during my time in the laboratory. <u>It is a certainty that all forensic chemists will make errors, whether administrative or technical in nature.</u> Laboratory processes should be such that systematic administrative and technical errors are prevented and random error are identified and corrected quickly and effectively. The laboratory must have procedures in place to identify such nonconformities and correct them <u>prior to issuing laboratory reports</u>. In the event that errors are detected <u>after</u> a laboratory report is issued, the laboratory must also have a procedure to address this situation.
<u>Critical Finding</u> – 100% peer review should be conducted prior to the issuance of any other drugs. Peer review should be conducted <u>on-site, by a competent, proficiency tested analyst.</u> Travel to a remote location for peer review is: inefficient, does not allow for rapid correction of nonconformities and subsequent case turn around, nor does it allow for potential on-site assessment of quality records, the physical evidence, BEST bag, etc. by the individual conducting the peer review.
<u>Critical Finding</u> – of the 12 cases reviewed, 58% had instances of broken chain of custody-i.e. COC documentation was improperly completed). While this was not due to drug chemist procedures, I note it here because a broken chain

of custody would/should prevent the drug results from being accepted by the courts and review of the chain of custody documentation should be a component of the laboratory's peer review process.
<u>I encourage the agency to conduct in-house training of Evidence and Property Room staff and submitting officers on this issue</u> and to require a proper COC prior to marijuana and other drug testing.

6) *Proficiency Testing*
Ms. Frazier participates in an external proficiency program (Collaborative Testing Services (CTS), Drug Analysis) on a semi-annual basis. I reviewed her latest proficiency test documentation which was thorough, complete, and accurate. <u>She is to be commended for her participation and test results, given that participation in external proficiency testing is voluntary for unaccredited laboratories.</u>

7) *Training/Professional Development*
I reviewed Ms. Frazier's training and professional development history while at CPD. She is to commended for her participation in the DEA Special Training Seminar for Drug Chemists and the two Agilent-sponsored GC/MS Training Courses. She has also attended local forensic drug chemistry meetings.
<u>Critical Finding</u> - I feel that Ms. Frazier should have additional focused intensive training in certain aspects of forensic drug chemistry. This would not only lead to overall process

improvement, but would give her the confidence that she needs to handle casework, troubleshoot instrumentation, understand theory and forensic terminology, etc. (Refer to Staffing comments below.)

Forensic drug chemists are required to receive twenty hours of documented continuing education each year (Refer to the Scientific Working Group for the Analysis of Seized Drug Guidelines (SWGDRG)). Continuing education can be achieved in a variety of ways (web-based, conferences, training courses). On-going continuing education is critical to cutting edge analysis, enhanced technical expertise and effective operations.

8) *Records/Laboratory Documents/Procedures*
   Critical Finding – long term storage of laboratory records should be in a secure, <u>climate controlled</u> environment (e.g. Iron Mountain, in house location).
   Ms. Frazier has a laboratory standard operating procedures (SOP) manual and is currently developing a chemical hygiene plan. She is to be commended. <u>A review/assessment of these documents was beyond the scope of this gap analysis.</u> The SOP should be reviewed by a qualified drug chemist for consistency with current lab practices and should be revised to include best practice recommendations (e.g. SWGDRG). Review and revision should be conducted on at least an annual basis.

9) *Staffing*
   Critical Finding – the daily operations (case load) and quality and safety practices required in this laboratory <u>extend beyond the capabilities of</u>

Commitment, Service and Betrayal

one analyst. A search for another qualified, experienced forensic drug chemist should be initiated as soon as possible. It is strongly recommended that this individual have:
Bachelor of Science (BS) degree from an accredited institution with 10 years' experience in GC/MS, IR instrumentation, from a high-volume laboratory, preferably ABC-certified, or, Master of Science (MS) degree from an accredited institution with at least 5-7 years' experience in GC/MS, IR instrumentation, from a high-volume laboratory, preferably ABC-certified and,
Refer to SWGDRG for additional, specific personnel prerequisites

Critical Finding – the above-described employee would supervise the laboratory's daily operations in all of its facets; Ms. Frazier would report to this individual on the organizational chart; her employee evaluation would also be conducted by this individual. Additional training, mentoring and peer review would also be facilitated with this arrangement.

I appreciate the opportunity to assist the agency with its path toward process improvement. I would like to extend my sincere appreciation Ms. Frazier for her invaluable assistance and her professionalism during my evaluation. She has accomplished much during her time at the agency. With additional structure and support, I am confident that she and her colleague(s) will be able to meet and exemplify best practice forensic chemistry guidelines.

This audit was taken in good faith with plans to improve the management of resources by implementing good scientific practices to move toward accreditation in the future. Unbeknownst to me, this audit would be the tool to discredit me and all that I was trying to achieve over the past three years. At the same time, this was the plan for RSCD to gain control over CPD. Since they could not use racial discrimination tactics as well as obstacles such as the removal of SLED training, member of the PORS retirement system as well as job functional tools (vehicle, cell phone and clothing allowance), the next step would be to close the laboratory and put blame on the person with the least control over the mechanisms (decision making) of the laboratory. It should also be noted that the status of the critical findings was prevalent and in place when the outgoing chemist was manager over the laboratory. The purpose of the audit was to highlight these situations because the command staff would not take my assessments, so the plan was to use someone else, who was supposed to be more creditable. Unbeknownst, the knife (daggers) were moving into my back. Even though the audit would highlight exceptions in my favor, the command staff would only use the negative aspects of the audit to further disrespect me with no common courtesy and professionalism.

25. The week of July 20th, 2014, the solicitor's office had requested to perform concurrent analyses with an outside laboratory from the Charleston area. Shockingly, the weights were different from the original weight. The timing for this event was not good but looking back on the situation... it further outlined the Evidence and Property Room storage deficiencies and not the laboratory. A reason to not suspect the laboratory because cases are only kept in the laboratory for a few weeks during analyses. Per conversations with the Property Room Manager, the

storage areas had to deal with the elements of the universe (heat, cold and humidity). This storage facility was not temperature controlled and documentation logbooks to record the daily temperature readings were none existent.

On another note, following the direction from another Lieutenant, I requested other cases from the evidence/property room with similar weights and chemical substances to check for a pattern. After making a request for several cases, at least several of the cases had drugs that had mold in them, a plastic storage bag was torn and the drugs were hard and dry (not of the consistency when analyzed) and the weight was different from the original analyses.

26. On July 21, 2014, per Captain, a memo was sent for all evidence submitted for analysis will be sent to SLED. (Note: **I never received this memo but was told that it was issued).** At this time marijuana will be separated from the hard drugs and analyzed at CPD. All marijuana case will continue to be analyzed at CPD and peer reviewed by me. Being shocked by this occurrence, this is the only change from the information from this audit. As I was presented in the audit as incompetent, but the laboratory was presented as meeting the standard.

27. On August 5, 2014, County lab director and drug analyst had audit at least 40 of the 200-plus cases that were pending peer review. For the next several weeks, the county lab director was requesting information (documentation) of my SOP and training. This was to be another part of their plan to further discredit my character and capabilities.

28. On August 21, 2014 at 11:00 am, I was called to a meeting with Captain and Sergeant and was told the all

drug analyses would cease in the laboratory. This was a directive from the Chief (at this time a new chief was hired on April 2014 and the interim chief had resigned). Based on this information, I was told that I can look into a lateral move to another department (referencing to positions at the COC-wastewater facility) or look for employment outside of the department. Due to the fact that Captain did know the timeframe, he would inquire and schedule a meeting with the chief. Unfortunately, the Captain was not able to make this happen.

29. On August 21, 2014 at 12:15 pm, the memo in the form of an email was issued throughout the department that all drug analyses will cease at CPD and all cases would be sent to SLED.

30. On August 22, 2014, I sent an e-mail to Chief Holbrook's administrative assistant to request a meeting. At 1:30 pm, I was summoned to the meeting. In attendance to the meeting were two department Majors, Captain and the Chief. Per the Chief, "the elephant is out in the room" and it must be dealt with." Per the memo about the laboratory, I will have the option to seek employment within or outside the city but there would not be a specific timeframe, but he did not want it to extend by six (6) months. Per information about the positions at the wastewater plant, they would look into a lateral move by talking with the supervisors in this area.

31. On the evening of August 22, 2014, my husband, who had a great love for boil peanuts (southern delicacy) that are cooked in a pressure cooker, outside in the backyard. While he was outside, I decided to get ready for bed. While walking passing the television in the

bedroom, WIS-TV news was coming on and the first story of the night to catch my attention was this story. At this point, loud and upset, I began calling my husband to come to see the news story. Both of us were in total amazement. Shockingly, there was my name in the story that had continued for at least two weeks as well as the news crawl (feed) running across the bottom of the television stations. To this date, I have never seen this happen to anyone in the news such as to what happened in this situation. At one point, a photograph was presented showing a picture from the department's employee file with numbers across the bottom that was televised and printed as though I were a criminal.

Over the weekend of August 22 thru August 24, 2014, several press releases from the television stations, WIS-TV and WLTX along with the State and Columbia Times newspapers were issued discussing the state of the crime laboratory. To the greatest shock in the history of my career, I was blamed for the closure of the laboratory and all of the deficiencies that were outlined in the impromptu audit. Later, I would find out from legal discovery documents that the press release had come from the Columbia Police Department to WIS-TV news station.

32. August 25, 2014, I was summoned to meet with the Chief. In attendance at this meeting were the Major, Captain and Deputy Chief (who was a lieutenant when I was hired in 2011 as well as involved with the training concerns with the laboratory). Per the Chief, the lateral move to the wastewater plant was no longer an option. At this time, I only had two (2) options. They were to resign that will be effective in two (2) weeks or to be terminated to be effective immediately. The timeframe to make a decision must be made in a

couple of hours or by the end of the day therefore subsequently, I had chosen to resign.

Written Letter of Resignation:

Per conversation with the Chief with attendees, Captain, Major and Deputy Chief and based on the options of choice, I have chosen to resign from this position as Drug Chemist to be effective September 12, 2014.

Not trusting these evil people, I did not desire or wanted a position with them. They did not know that I already had another position with a company in a neighboring county. The company was a leading manufacturer of pharmaceutical and other over the counter medication in the United States. A week after leaving, I started working as a Quality Control Chemist in a management capacity. This was a position of a lifetime that would lead to so many opportunities.

While working there, I would attend weekly quality meetings as well as daily protocols for the quality control laboratory. She was one of the chemists who managed another quality control lab. She also was as on the board that interviewed for this position. She said, "During your interview I was so impressed by the attitude, charisma and manner that you presented." She wished and hoped that someday she would grow to be the same way.

While overwhelmed by the compliment, I thanked her.. All of this was short lived. While driving home from work, I received a call from the contract company that performed the hiring for the pharmaceutical company. He stated that the company had felt that I was not a good fit for them. As strange as it could be, I was not so understandably hurt. On this day at work, I had participated in the weekly quality control meeting for the entire plant as well as asked if I could work overtime for the next several weeks. Looking back, the situation with the police department announcement from news stations and newspapers had led to another lost opportunity.

*Read the Press Releases from the CPD, the RCSD Department and local news stations and newspapers along with my Personal Responses that are written in (**Bold**)*

Holbrook looks to move ahead, answer questions about drug lab

By Jack Kuenzie on September 02, 2014

COLUMBIA, SC WIS) -

After taking over as Columbia Police Chief in April, Skip Holbrook said he would launch a top-to-bottom exam of the department's operations.

The audit, which began in May, uncovered a backlog of drug cases analyzed by the city's only chemist, but they were in need of a second opinion before they could be taken to court.

That touched off events including a sharply-worded critique of the lab by the Richland County Sheriff's Department, the closing of the lab and, a week ago, the resignation of analyst Brenda Frazier. Since then, the city has asked experts from the Richland

County Sheriff's Department to review about 190 cases as Holbrook attempts to remedy the part of his department that wasn't working very well.

Response:

What makes RCSD capable of performing laboratory audits? They are only certified by ASCLD to perform analyses that are listed on their certification. To perform a fair assessment, audits are performed by an outside agency (independent party) who will not gain in the outcome of the audit. This is a conflict of interest on RCSD involvement in the situations especially since they are to benefit from the outcome (obtaining control of the crime laboratory and/or eventually the entire police department).

"I've made every attempt to stay very positive and forward thinking and I don't think it's productive to dwell on the past, " Holbrook said. "However, when situations such as this come up, I think sometimes I understand you know how we need to move forward to be able to digest what got you there to begin with."

The methodology, safety for personnel and even security were among the problems identified in the Richland County report. The audit even suggested the police department did not have a current inventory of drug evidence or a clear idea of who had access to the lab. Holbrook says those issues have already been resolved.

Response:

How was this issue resolved? …. With the forced resignation of the only chemist? SLED methodology (dated 2004/2005) was utilized for drug analysis but they never refer to this in any of the press releases. In July 2014, I received the updated methodology from SLED. As for safety (fume hood, fire extinguisher, chemical showers and storages and ventilation), the laboratory was in this condition upon my arrival. CPD only started to make changes after the GAP

analysis. Security (individuals with access to the evidence in the bank vault) had been a problem that I discussed with Sergeant and Captain.

"I'm very comfortable with our accounting of individual access to the lab and how we categorize log and store evidence," Holbrook said.

Response:

What steps were in place to make this happen?

As the days continue, Holbrook continues to solve problems that began long before he moved to Columbia.

Response:

Problems that were there before my arrival as well as I tried to help to alleviate some of the problems but did not receive support from the command staff.

"People are going to make mistakes in this business and, to me," Holbrook said, "what gives us credibility is, in situations where we do you got to own up to them and demonstrate why they're not going to happen again. That's how you restore public confidence.

Response:

What people are going to make mistakes? I was not given the platform (voice and/or support) to make the necessary changes to prevent this type of situation from occurring. Chief Holbrook is allowed to make mistakes with no repercussions, but I am to become the sacrificial lamb for problems/situation before my arrival as well as to not be given the support to make the necessary changes.

Holbrook says his goal is to build world-class department that includes a better city-operated drug lab. However, the reality dictates certain limits on what the city can afford.

Future of Columbia Police Department's drug analysis lab still unclear

By Jack Kuenzie, September 3, 2014

COLUMBIA, SC (WIS) -

It has been several days since the Columbia Police Department's drug analysis lab was shut down and nearly 200 cases handed over to the Richland County Sheriff's Department.

Some city leaders would like the police department to beef up its own capabilities and resources.

Others suggest it might be best to partner with other agencies including the Richland County Sheriff's Department.

Still there are many unresolved questions as city officials try to sort out the mess involving operations of the police department's drug lab.

Columbia police Chief Skip Holbrook, summed up his first 21 weeks in charge of the often-troubled department.

"I feel like I've been you know, juggling bowling balls since I've been here," Holbrook said at a council committee meeting Wednesday.

One of the toughest challenges for Holbrook so far has been trying to figure out how his agency managed to process hundreds of drug possession cases with only one chemist on staff.

Response:

Who did he ask? Until August 22, 2014, I have never spoken with Chief Holbrook.

Normally, there would be two.

Response:

In the history of CPD, they had never employed two (2) chemists. Through conversations with HR representative, I believe that they used me to get rid of the outgoing chemist because of their issues with her. On several conversations with one of the crime scene technician, she was told that this department will never have two chemists. This crime scene technician had expressed interest for this position but was denied the opportunity.

But in June 2012, the city's senior analyst, Melissa Hendricks, quit the job she'd held for more than eight years.

Response:

She quit due to issues with the department before my arrival. During the interview process, I did not see the laboratory or the outgoing chemist until taking on the chemist position. During the six (6) months working with her, she expressed this concern numerous times. After reviewing her credentials from legal reporting documents, she has a bachelor of science degree in science, so does this make her a chemist without a degree in chemistry.

Police say there was personal conflict with her junior co-worker, Brenda Frazier.

Response:

Where is the ownership in this statement? Who are the police? What are the personal conflicts? Why did she have personal conflicts with her junior co-worker? For obvious reasons, Hendricks was not included in the hiring process therefore she was not going to be included in the training process therefore leaving a disaster for the incoming chemist.

Hendricks' departure left a vacancy that is still unfilled.

Response:

Hendricks left June 22, 2012. The position was advertised for a short period of time after she had left but was removed. On May 8, 2014, the position was posted again after the arrival of Chief Holbrook. If the department had taken notice of the problem (backlog and peer review concerns), why did they wait almost two (2) years to address the concerns/issues?

That's a problem because drug cases need peer review or a second opinion to hold up in court.

With the opening review of Columbia cases was turned over to a regional pool, but that effort disintegrated again due in part to what Holbrook calls Frazier's inability to accept criticism.

Response:

The regional pool disintegrated due to the fact that this peer review team were colleagues of the outgoing chemist and they had issues with the hiring and training process of the new chemist (Brenda Frazier) just as did the outgoing chemist.

Frazier resigned after Holbrook closed the lab, leaving hundreds of cases under new scrutiny.

Response:

Not true. Frazier resigned a month after the closing of the laboratory. Prior to the resignation, Frazier was involved in peer review of marijuana cases as well as analyzing other cases. Several (200) cases were under review and not scrutiny. Per direction from Captain Oree, Frazier was told to continue drug analyses while a peer review solution would be developed by the command staff.

About 190 of those cases are being re-tested by the Richland County Sheriff's Department, an arrangement Mayor Steve Benjamin suggested Wednesday should be further explored.

Commitment, Service and Betrayal

"It's in the best interests not just of the people of Columbia but in this region to find ways to work together on every project," said Columbia Mayor Steve Benjamin. "This is obviously an opportunity."

Others on council said a solution may be simpler.

Councilman Moe Baddourah said the city should just hire two new chemist.

"The actual system works," Baddourah said. "And it's designed to work within the court system and the prosecutors and the judges. So why change that? Why can't you just find two chemists?"

Holbrook said that's not as easy as it appears.

The senior chemist opening hasn't produced a candidate since the chief got it posted May 8.

Formalizing a partnership with the county would give the city time to look at a long-term plan that might involve turning property on Busby Street in north Columbia into a police facility that could include a more advanced drug lab.

Response:

This was the obvious objective from the beginning but to use Brenda Frazier as the sacrificial lamb for RCSD ultimate plan.

EDITORIAL: COLUMBIA, SC'S FAILED DRUG LAB SHOULD BE ABSORBED INTO RICHLAND COUNTY'S STELLAR ONE

Read from the State Newspaper, August 28, 2014

Richland County, SC — COLUMBIA POLICE Chief Skip Holbrook wisely shuttered the department's drug lab amid disturbing news that its lone analyst wasn't properly trained and that evidence might have been mishandled, putting nearly 200 cases in jeopardy.

Response:

Who takes responsibility that the lone chemist was not properly trained? No one is addressing the fact the SLED would not perform training for CPD but trained the chemist for Horry County in 2013. I reached out to this chemist to use her for peer review in February/March 2014 but was told that she did not have court room experience and was too new to use for peer review. Per discussion with the Horry County Chemist, she reached out to other forensic chemist in the state and they would not peer review with her for the same reason. At the present time her cases were peer review by a department narcotics agent who is not technically qualified to peer review cases.

Why was evidence mishandled? Was it due to improper and/or antiquated storage systems?

How could 200 cases be in jeopardy when the this was the directive from Captain on 3/2014 to continue analyzing samples until a solution to the peer review situation could be determined?

It would be even wiser to keep the lab closed for good, especially since there is a much better alternative that should have been adopted long ago. Columbia's operation should be merged into the Richland County Sheriff's Department, whose lab is easily one of the best in the state. It has never made sense for the city and county to have redundant facilities.

Chief Holbrook and Columbia officials should waste no time petitioning Sheriff Leon Lott and Richland County leaders to merge the labs. Not only would it be more efficient and cost-effective; more importantly, it would assure that Columbia is getting high-quality analyses that prosecutors can feel confident presenting at trial.

As it stands, the city is conducting an internal audit of the drug analysis lab and will seek independent reviews of 188 cases. It's safe to assume that accused and convicted individuals will be raising questions about the validity of the evidence presented against them. And who could blame them? What if someone was accused and convicted on analyses that were flawed? Unfortunately, the monumental mess also could give opportunists who were rightly convicted an opening to cast doubt over evidence in their cases.

Quite frankly, the analyst, Brenda Frazier, got off lightly by being allowed to resign. But while Ms. Frazier, who assisted on nearly 800 cases since being employed in 2011, shoulders much of the blame, this isn't all her fault. Who was overseeing this division? Chief Holbrook and city officials must determine why the situation deteriorated to the point it did in Columbia's drug lab.

Response:

This needs to be defined that I got off lightly by resigning (forced termination). How was I assisted on nearly 800 cases and by whom? With all of the opposition, it was a major achievement to analyze and report 800 cases as well as the management of the laboratory.

Who was overseeing this division? Should it have been the Police Department Command Staff? As it can be seen, the only person to be held responsible was the lowest person on the team, Brenda Frazier

My input was never utilized to better understand the situation therefore I would ask questions about Chief Holbrook's management capabilities and methodology for handling any situation by leaving the City of Columbia open to a civil lawsuit.

The chief said that historically there were two chemists at the department, which allowed them to review one another's work for accuracy and quality. But shortly after Ms. Frazier joined the lab, she became its only chemist, and her work determining the weight and kind of drugs being tested was crucial in the prosecution of criminal drug cases. What led to Ms. Frazier becoming the alone analyst? Why wasn't another chemist hired? While she could go outside for peer review — and did, for a while — leaving her alone and apparently not closely supervised turned out to be a recipe for disaster.

Response:

Per Chief Holbrook, the department did not historically have two (2) chemists (never until the short time in the first six (6) months of 2012.

I become the only chemist due to the hiring/training methods and the outgoing chemist became angry and quit.

Another chemist was not hired because the management staff was under the impression that obtaining a regional peer teams would work just as it did for the outgoing chemist. They did not want to believe that this regional peer team had similar concern/issues with the outgoing chemist based on feedback from her while she was training, Brenda Frazier.

Close supervision was not the problem but having a supportive management staff would have help to alleviate the recipe for disaster.

Without a doubt, it could take some time to unravel this mess, which delivers yet another black eye to a department that has spent the past several years trying to recover from one body blow after another, from scandals to repeated changes in the chief's office.

Response:

This problem is part of the demise of the crime laboratory. There was so much internal fighting in the management staff until underlying problems in the laboratory was never expressed to the management staff. Upon arrival to CPD, the Deputy Chief, who had recommended hiring of Brenda Frazier, was fired. The Chief, who hired Brenda Frazier, had resigned for personal reasons as well as the interim chief had resigned for better opportunities. The Chief, who hired Brenda Frazier, as well as others such as a captain, interim chief, mayor and the assistant city manager were involved in an unethical scandal. Where was the time and personnel who could have concentrated on the situations with the Crime Laboratory?

But something good could come from this if city and county officials agree on a merged lab operated by the Sheriff's Department, an idea, the city leaders rejected more than a decade ago.

While the city chose to continue operating its own duplicative lab that grew into the embarrassment we see today, Richland County has built a top-notch facility since starting its operation back in 2000. Sheriff Lott insists the key to Richland's success is that he built the system the right way: Although Richland has a modern facility with cutting-edge technology, that wasn't the priority; instead, Sheriff Lott said, he focused on hiring highly trained, skilled experts more than capable of conducting credible drug analyses as well as ballistic and DNA testing.

We see no downside to Columbia transferring the funding and positions from its failed lab to the sheriff's department. It reduces duplication, improves the quality of analysis and furthers the goal of combining city and county services where possible to improve efficiency and control costs. This deal needs to be struck today.

Response:

The ultimate goal for RCSD and Sheriff Leon Lott. To date, 2/2018, this has not occurred and probably will not happen. It is all about who has control. As the rules of monopoly, the person who controls the dice, will have all of the power. This situation was all about power. As noted in the CPD audit, this question was asked, "Why is the Chief of Police's name on the Drug Enforcement Agency (DEA) Certification for Control Substances." Normally, the name on the license is the Laboratory Manager. This is the person who had received training and is certified by DEA. With hindsight being 20/20, since this was noted in the GAP analysis by RCSD lab director, I should have walked upstairs to the Chief's office and hand the reigns for him to continue the impromptu audit.

EXCLUSIVE: Columbia, Richland sheriff's crime labs planning merger

By JOHN MONK, August 29, 2014

Columbia police chief Skip Holbrook will merge his now-defunct small crime lab with the Richland County Sheriff's

Department's much larger and nationally accredited crime lab, The State has learned.

Response:

The ultimate goal for RCSD and Sheriff Leon Lott.

That move – likely to be announced next week – was discussed in a sheriff's department email viewed by The State newspaper. The merger was confirmed Friday by Mayor Steve Benjamin.

The merger will take place in the wake of recent disclosures that the city's small crime lab had possibly mishandled and improperly analyzed evidence in nearly 200 criminal drug cases. Holbrook closed down the crime lab Aug. 21. Its sole employee, analyst Brenda Frazier, has resigned.

Response:

These 200 cases are under peer review. Peer Review is a system that allows for coaching, mentoring and training for administrative and technical review of reports that adhere to scientific criteria that are outlined in standard operating procedures for each respective laboratory. While under peer review and based on the feedback, the reports can be changed for typographical and technical errors which may require repeating all of the analyses and/or re-typing the report.

After technical and scientific review, per response from Teresa Knox, City Attorney, had stated that there were not mishandling and improper analyses of evidence for any of the cases by Brenda Frazier. It was never confirmed that Brenda Frazier had mishandled or improperly analyzed evidence. These were allegation by persons who had no idea what was involved in the daily management responsibilities of the crime lab. The improprieties had occurred due to the

improper storage of the evidence. This was noted in the GAP analysis audit report that the command staff did not want to address. They had chosen to point the finger at the lowest person in the system instead of reviewing the entire broken system.

"Everyone wins – it's in the best interests of the people of the Midlands," Benjamin said. "It was Chief Holbrook's idea, and I appreciate the sheriff being open to it as well."

Response:

Really!!! Is this truly Chief Holbrook's idea or the ultimate goal/plan of Sheriff Leon Lott? As 02/2018, neither this plan or the new CPD crime lab plans have come to fruition.

Benjamin said he and a few top-level city officials met with Holbrook Tuesday at City Hall, "and he indicated a strong interest in establishing a central crime lab and a partnership with the sheriff. He felt strongly it would be a good partnership that would save the taxpayers' dollars and give us all the opportunity to work together in a meaningful way."

Besides Benjamin, present at that meeting were Mayor Pro Tem Brian DeQuincey Newman, city attorney Teresa Knox and senior assistant city manager Allison Baker. City manager Teresa Wilson has been out all week and was not at that meeting.

"We directed Chief Holbrook to go ahead and establish a memorandum of understanding," Benjamin said.

Benjamin said City Council will be discussing matters such as the cost of the city's share of the crime lab tab. But he said spending on the scientific expertise needed to analyze and process evidence is one thing the city won't scrimp on.

Response:

When presenting ideas and solutions to Sergeant, my direct supervision, I have been told the city will not pay for this therefore he would tear up the requisition and/or just leave it on his desk and not turn it into his supervision. I have been told so many times that if it does not cost money then I can move forward with the idea. For example, the calibration of weights for the balances that was performed by the SC Metrology Laboratory for free.

"There are certain things that a 21st-century municipality ought to be willing to pay for," Benjamin said. "We will work on those details."

The council's public safety committee – made up of Newman and council members Sam Davis and Cameron Runyan – likely will take up the topic at Wednesday's meeting at City Hall. Then, in mid-September, the full council will likely discuss it at a regular meeting, Benjamin said.

Earlier this week, Richland County Sheriff Leon Lott – who was in discussions with Holbrook about the merger – sent a confidential email to county officials, including county council members.

"In the next couple of days, the Columbia police chief will announce he is partnering with the Richland County Sheriff's Department in our forensic lab," Lott wrote in his email in an effort to keep his council members informed.

Although Lott declined on Friday to comment on the email, he acknowledged that he and Holbrook were "obviously in serious discussions," adding, "Any further comment on a formal arrangement would more appropriately come from the city."

Chief Holbrook did not make himself available for comment, but a spokeswoman confirmed that Lott and Holbrook have had "multiple discussions" for more than a month on the city drug lab operations. "They continue to work together in future strategies," the spokeswoman said.

In Lott's email, he said his crime lab "will start with testing of their drugs, and over time move toward ballistics examination, crime scene processing and finally DNA."

Lott's lab is nationally and internationally accredited and has numerous specialties. His experts process crime scenes, collect and store all kinds of evidence as well as analyze drugs, fingerprints, DNA, ballistics and firearms. The county lab also has an expanding DNA database that can give "quick hits" in focusing on likely suspects.

Evidence from crime labs is an essential part of most criminal cases. Only if the evidence has been properly handled and evaluated can a defendant be convicted of a crime. Evidence also can exonerate a suspect. All evidence introduced in criminal court cases is subject to rigorous scrutiny by defense lawyers.

Richland County Coroner Gary Watts, whose investigators often are at crime scenes, said in the areas his workers interact with Lott's – crime scene analysis and drug matters – Lott's experts have "the highest standards and methods, and their practices are above reproach."

Fifth Circuit Solicitor Dan Johnson, whose prosecutors have used results from both crime labs, was not available for comment.

Response:

To date, 03/2018, none of these ideas have come to fruition. This is evident of the problems that I experienced of working

for change with very little and/or no support. Dan Johnson, Fifth Circuit Solicitor for Richland and Kershaw Counties, had written a letter to the South Carolina Bar association and noted that cases that were analyzed and reported from Brenda Frazier will not be used until a complete investigation takes place. The investigation had been completed and noted by Teresa Knox, City of Columbia attorney, that the proper protocols were utilized and the cases are in good standing. To date, no letter has been addressed to the South Carolina bar association with these findings. On 3/20/2018, Dan Johnson was accused of the misappropriation of funds from the narcotic seizure account (value to at least $300,000) for personal expenditures. To date, no personal comments or letter to the SC Bar association had been issued to address this concern.

On September 18, 2018 as reported in the State Newspaper by John Monk, Fifth Circuit Solicitor Dan Johnson, one of 16 prosecutors in South Carolina, was indicted by a federal grand jury on 26 fraud charges that are connected to allegations that he misappropriated more than $55,000 in taxpayer money. He was charged with 26 counts of wire fraud, mail fraud, conspiracy and theft of government money. These charges carry penalties of 10 to 20 years in prison and fines of up to $250,000 for each count.

Richland County Council members contacted by The State had generally favorable reactions to a possible merger of Lott's and the city's crime lab operations.

"We're very proud of our lab," said council member Greg Pearce. "It's one of the unknown shining stars of our county." The sheriff's lab can process a variety of kinds of evidence much faster than if the evidence were to be processed by SLED's lab, which handles evidence from all over the state, he said.

"The lab is underutilized now," he said. "We can do a lot more without adding tremendous cost."

Council member James Manning said, "The more opportunity we have to work collaboratively between the county and any municipality in the county has great potential for the citizens."

Council member Seth Rose said a merger would be "a huge step forward" for law local enforcement. "Consolidation will be a good deal for taxpayers and help public safety. This isn't just about drug analysis – it's about all kinds of crimes and solving them faster and better."

Benjamin, in a letter publicly released Friday, said he wants city council to have a full briefing on what led to the failure of the city's crime lab. In the letter, to council public safety committee chairman Newman, Benjamin said he wanted to "collect all the facts" behind the drug lab's closing "so that we and the people can clearly understand how this happened, what could have been done to prevent it, what is the potential impact to our city and citizens and what are we doing now to both minimize that impact and ensure that a situation like this never happens again. Let's leave no stone unturned."

<u>City leaders rejected the idea of merged labs more than a decade ago</u>. But the city and county cooperate in several areas of government service to residents.

Response:

The crime laboratory was in the same situation over ten (10) years ago. The outgoing chemist was new to the crime

laboratory with the same analytical equipment and property/evidence storage area. At this time, they did not want to merge. WHY?

The county owns and manages a library system and the jail, which is used by the city and various municipalities. The city runs an animal shelter used by the county as well as a joint-use fire department.

<u>During a leadership vacancy at its police force two years ago, city council seriously considered a merger of some sort with Lott's department, touting it as a way to save taxpayers money and operate more efficiently. But the idea failed in a close, surprise vote.</u>

Response:

Why did the vote fail and based on what information?

Exclusive: Columbia Police hired chemist despite warning from sheriff experts, Lott says

The State Newspaper by Clif Leblanc

Sheriff Lott states that the Columbia Police asked forensic scientist to evaluate and interview three finalists for the police department job. Frazier was among the three.

Response:

On the date in question, there were only two (2) people interviewing before this panel. On the panel was Demetra Garvin, Andy Farmer, Grey Amick, Missy Horne and Tera (Not sure of her last name). Per Felicia Heath, CPD-HR, the panel of questions were not weighted fairly and I was chosen as the better candidate. Per Demetra Garvin, I would be up to speed on drug analysis within six (6) to nine (9) months. This was told to Brenda Frazier by Felicia Heath from Demetra Garvin, RCSD expert and lab director.

On Dec. 1, 2011, the reviewers endorsed the two others as qualified for the job, Lott said. They recommended that Frazier, then known as Brenda Jenkins, not to be hired, Lott said.

Response:

This is the first time that I had heard this information. Why did they hire Brenda Frazier? Was it not because I had the most knowledge and experience of the two candidates.

City administrators on Wednesday said that they were examining employment records and did not respond to the newspaper's inquiry about why Frazier was hired.

Response:

This is the first time that I had heard this information but leads to speculation that this was the plan from the beginning to ultimately take over the crime lab as well as to use tactics to discredit and disrespect, Brenda Frazier.

Chief Holbrook states that peer review is a required lab procedure that provides for ways to double check drug evaluations, including the exact weight of a drug.

Response:

Not true. Peer review is a required process that a laboratory can use and/or not based on their respective laboratory's standard operating procedures. There are several laboratories in SC that do not perform peer review at all such as Florence and York Counties (until July 2014). Peer review cannot verify the exact weight of a drug. This can only be done by actual presence in the respective laboratory while the weight of the substance is being determined. The peer review can only check the calculation and conversion factors to determine ounces and grains.

But by February of this year, Frazier was dropped from the peer system, "due to her inability to accept criticism and resistance in conforming to the group's methodologies, wrote the chief.

Response:

Regional peer review begun in 11/2012 by contacting Lexington County Sheriff Department's chemist, who did want to participate because of personal reasons. For weeks, Sergeant was trying to reach this department for a date/time to start peer review, but no one would return his telephone calls. Since hearing of the situation, I suggested to the Sergeant that I would call Aiken County's chemist for input on the matter. After speaking with Aiken Counties' chemist, she agreed after speaking with the other two chemists and told me to meet them that Friday for peer review.

On March 2014 per Lexington and Orangeburg Counties' chemist, I was verbally told that they do not have to peer review with me per directives from their command staff. To my surprise and telling my command staff, they were shocked to hear this. Sergeant and Lieutenant had met with Aiken and Lexington Counties on two (2) occasion and they assume that they had come to an agreement to peer review with CPD. Per Sergeant, Lexington county's chemist is crazy and very difficult to work with. Per Sergeant, I was told that the peer review team had a problem with the way in which I hired and trained for this chemist position. The regional peer team questioned the method of training from the retired head of SLED's forensic lab. The regional peer team was of the mindset that she had been away from the discipline to long to be qualified in training anyone even though she is the department chair for the forensic science program for Morris College.

As for Chief Holbrook hearing about the situation with the difference in the weight of the crack cocaine and therefore closing the laboratory; this situation happened on Tuesday, July 22, 2014. He closed (cease all drug analysis) the laboratory on August 21, 2014 which was almost a month later.

The first laboratory audit was on Friday, July 11, 2014 by RCSD. On Monday, July 21, 2014, the marijuana analyst and I were told that SLED will analyze all hard drug cases and marijuana case will be analyzed at CPD. All marijuana cases will be peer reviewed by the chemist before issue. (We were told that a memo was issued to the department per the Captain, but I had never seen the memo). Per Sergeant, I was to complete all open cases but do not open new case. The last day that I performed analyses on laboratory instrumentation was 7/31/2014. On August 5, 2014, I was told that RCSD was coming to peer review the 200 plus cases that were still open. The reason for 200 plus cases accumulation was due to not having the ability to have them peer reviewed. Per direction from the Captain on 3/2014, he was working on a plan to have the cases peer reviewed. I was not aware that there was another audit until reading about it in the newspaper.

Holbrook is seeking to hire chemist:

Response:

The first panel of interviews (Brenda Frazier was on the board interview) took place on June 27, 2014 and second panel of interviews on July 29, 2014 and position was advertised since May 8, 2014. If there was such a serious problem, why was the interview process taking so long. As for the three candidates, they are less qualified than Brenda Frazier, so if they were told by RCSD experts not to hire Brenda Frazier then why did Chief Holbrook consider these three candidates? Due to the fact that CPD took so long to make a decision, one of the most qualified and trained candidate (RCSD chemist who resigned in 5/2014 from RCSD) who interviewed for this position but decided to take a position with another company.

It is not true that this position was vacant since 2012. The advertisement for this position did not happen until after

Chief Holbrook's arrival in April 2014. The advertisement did not appear on the COC website until May 2014.

CHEMIST (COLUMBIA POLICE DEPARTMENT) , May 7, 2014

Term: Regular Full-Time
Pay: $45,223 - $59,790/ANNUAL

Nature of Work:
The purpose of this position is to perform responsible professional and technical work in the chemical analysis of drugs and other substances held as evidence in criminal cases; to assist with other criminal evidence analysis, and to perform related work as required.

Qualifications:
Bachelor's degree in chemistry, or closely related field with six (6) months' work experience in developing methods and procedures for the effective and efficient analysis of drugs and other substances confiscated by Police Department officers and held as evidence in criminal cases.

Special Requirements:
Must possess and maintain a valid SC Class "D" Driver's License and have an acceptable driving record. Must have knowledge of personal computer equipment with skill in the use of Microsoft Office preferred, utilizing Outlook, spreadsheet and presentation software programs as well as data entry skills. Must possess and maintain or be able to obtain SLED certification within one (1) year from date of hire or promotion. Preference may be given to applicants who currently possess SLED/Drug

Analysis certification. Preference may be given to applicants who are a current Class I Law Enforcement Officer.

This is the same advertisement that was issued when I interviewed and was hired in 12/27/2011. The underlined sentence in the advertisement was required but CPD could not obtain SLED training. I was told that SLED does not offer this training anymore but the chemist, from Horry County, was trained in 2013 after I was hired by CPD in 2011. When I had given this information to the Sergeant, he had thrown his pencil across his desk and said, "Politics".

Chief Holbrook, "The department must hire qualified chemists and not lower its standard to fill the jobs quickly and We can't deviate from the standard just to put a butt in a seat"

Response:

What standard is he referring to? By the City of Columbia Human Resources department, I was deemed qualified for the position at CPD as well as the City of Columbia-Water and Wastewater departments therefore are these departments lowering/deviating from their standards of hiring. CPD had knowledge of my education and experiences coming into this position. They made the decision to hire and offered training by the outgoing chemist, SLED and Morris College. To the best of my ability, I worked through all the challenges and obstacles to provide a service as well as to become an asset to the department if they so desire to do their due diligence to meet the objectives from the chemist's advertisement.

As noted from these press releases and prior of the CPD's contact with the news stations and the newspapers, no one talked with me from the City of Columbia Council as well as the command staff.

With many conversations with Demi Garvin, RSCD lab director, we discussed the conditions in the CPD laboratory where she agreed to help with the problems. To my knowledge the Chief stated that he found out about the problems from the laboratory through a conversation with Sheriff Leon Lott who discussed it with Demetra Garvin of RCSD. Per my discussion with her, she was to talk with Leon Lott to help improve conditions at CPD because I had been unsuccessful over the past two (2) years. Looking back from where I am now, this was the beginning of the plan to take over the laboratory by RSCD. As it does appear, I would have become the sacrificial lamb to put their plan to work in their favor.

Commitment, Service and Betrayal

Resignation and Seeking Justice

Now the legal fight begins with trying to find an attorney to take on the City and the Police Department as well as gaining the knowledge about the disparaging people that I had the opportunity of working with for the past three years. Over the -past several years, this attorney, who I assumed to have my best interest, was only the snake in the grass. Throughout all the events with the city, I would use his legal advice and expertise. Not realizing that he had alternative reasons such as to gain an inside track on the many occurrences within the department as well as to use this information to gain access or a chance to become the city attorney. On the day that I had resigned, I called him. What a BIG mistake!!! His first response was why did you resign and stated that I should have allowed them to terminate me.

At this point I had become weary of his advice but made an appointment to see him the next day. This point always comes to mind, I had never reached out for his advice and he did not return my calls. He was always receptive to the calls and for good reason that I have learned over the past several years. As well as on the last day with the city, I had spoken with the retired chemist from SLED and the chemist from the coastal area. To this date, I have not heard or spoken with either of them. What does this show about their true intentions? This represents the old historical tale that was spoken by my mother. During the times of assistance and help from true coaches, mentors and friends, they are forever present. Like roaches, when the light is switched on in a dark room... they scatter in any hole or crevice for cover. Right now, this has been said nicely without the characteristic superlatives.

The colloquial term for these types of people is "frenemies." My husband and I met with this attorney to discuss the next course of action. He is trying to determine if the chemist position with the city would be classified as a public figure. Under the South Carolina Tort Claims Act, a person cannot sue for compensation for defamation of character if the person is classified as a public figure. Astonished once again, the thoughts of a public figure would be an elected official, where as I was not elected to this position. If this was not a blow to the case, he also stated that he could not act as the attorney due to the fact that he was representing the city and county on insurance claims cases. This representation would present a conflict of interest with his law firm. Later I would find out that this was not the real reason because his law firm was working on obtaining the city and county as the sole attorney. During this time, he was sending me to other attorneys who would never return the calls and/or expressed that they did not handle civil cases of this nature.

While watching the news on the case for another Captain with this municipality, my husband and I made the decision to reach out to this individual's attorney. We reached out to him and he called on a Sunday afternoon to schedule a meeting the next day. What an interesting conversation we had the next day!!! He heard of my case and the first impression in his words of what the general public and the city was stating about me, "Here is this African American woman who could not do her job and is blaming the city." Currently, I am putting it nicely by not using the characteristic superlatives. He also spoke of the case with the Captain and using a reporter from a local news station to present the case to the public. This Captain had a taped conversation between himself and other city officials that would be detrimental if the information was leaked to the public. To keep this information away from the public, the city had settled this case before it turned into a lawsuit. Unfortunate for my case, this reporter (Jody Barr) had moved on and notably so because he was very good. What I mean by good is that he would investigate a story for the real truth. Rumor had it that he not only moved on, but this establishment did not want him around because of his tenacity and due diligence to find the truth.

After discussing the cost to take on this case, we moved forward on putting together the lawsuit against the city of Columbia and a new conference. The date for the new conference was December 16, 2014. Below is the statement that I had read at the news conference:

TOOMER-FRAZIER VS. CITY OF COLUMBIA
PRESS CONFERENCE NOTES

On December 27, 2011, I started working with the Columbia Police Department as a forensic drug chemist. Effective, September 12, 2014, the Chief of Police for the City of Columbia gave me the option of resigning or face termination. Accepting the most logical option, I resigned, not because I wanted to but because it was the only reasonable option of choice. Despite my resignation, the Columbia Police Department viciously and intentionally destroyed my good name by falsely communicating to the public that I

was the cause of **all** the problems in the drug lab. This false communication has severely damaged my good name and decreased my marketability as a forensic chemist and chemist.

On November 03, 2014, I filed suit against the City of Columbia because I refuse to let anyone rob me of my good name without a legal fight.

My allegations against the Columbia Police Department are straightforward and very provable. The law says that I had to right to make and enforce the terms and conditions of my employment contract with the City of Columbia on the same terms and conditions as white employees. That did not happen. My lawyer has carefully stated the facts in the complaint. Is this case about race? Absolutely. Let me emphasize just a few points why I believe that this case is about race and retaliation.

POINTS TO EMPHASIZE

- The City of Columbia did not give me the right to select my own peer review team. Peer review teams are critical because no drugs analysis results can be released by the department unless it has been peered reviewed. To my knowledge, the white forensic chemists before me could select their own peer review teams.
- When I was initially hired, I was classified as a Class III Police Officer. This is important because it affects retirement benefits. In March 2013, I was informed by the City that I would no longer serve as a Class III Police Officer under the Police Officer Retirement System (PORS). Due to the removal out of the Police Retirement

system had caused a reduction of my salary in the amount of $2826.00. This did not happen to the white chemists.

- Under the City's policy, all drug analyses were required to be peer reviewed before being released by the City. However, the drug analysis by the white analyst who performed analysis on the marijuana was released without peer review.

I was denied the SLED (Forensic Science) required training that other similarly situated and provided to white drug chemists.

What catalyst caused my forced termination? The Chief of the Columbia Police Department requested the Richland County Sheriff Department, through Demetra ("Demi" Garvin) conduct an evaluation of the drug analysis department. The evaluation is referred to as a "gap analysis". I was not given any advanced notice of the evaluation. Demi Garvin just magically appeared on July 11, 2014 and commenced the evaluation of the drug analysis department. At the start of the evaluation, Garvin urged me to tell her everything because the evaluation could serve as a lightning rod to send help to my department. Based upon Garvin's encouragement, I used the evaluation to point out all the things that required attention with the department, with the expectation that the evaluation would foster assistance from management to remedy some of the issues in my department. Let's talk about some of the things that were discussed with Demi Garvin:

THINGS THAT I TOLD GARVIN

- I informed Garvin that the white drug analyst who was responsible for analyzing marijuana was not required to have his work peer reviewed, in violation of protocol.
- I told her that the Columbia Police Department had failed to identify all individuals who had possession of keys to the laboratory and who had access to the large bank vault (storage vault which stored the drug evidence on a short-term basis) and (this vault contained the powdered controlled standards and drugs). This practice began February 2014 that was never implemented for the previous white drug chemists.
- I told her about the protocol to procure supplies and chemicals and she stated that it was taking too long to receive supplies from the time the order was placed until they are received.
- I told her about the policy and procedures for balance calibrations and she stated that the City was not properly calibrating its equipment (balances that are used to measure the amount of drugs) in the drug lab;
- I told her about the caseload which led her to conclude that the City did not have the laboratory department properly staffed in order to adequately accomplish its mission.

After I raised these issues with Garvin, the City of Columbia made me the scapegoat and hung me out to the media to dry. If I had just kept my mouth shut and just tolerated the inequalities, I would have still been working with the City of Columbia today. I made a conscious decision to bring these issues to Garvin attention, and I made a conscious decision to challenge my termination in Court. I would rather walk through Hell with gasoline on my shoulders rather than to take this injustice from the City of Columbia without a fight.

The City is intentionally misleading you to believe that I jeopardized over 200 cases, yet, not a single review has established any error. The 200 cases that the City mentioned in the media had not been peer reviewed. Therefore, any analysis that I performed on these cases were not ready for release—they were backlogged. More importantly, if every result had to be peer reviewed, how could I have make an error without the person peer reviewing my work also making an error by overlooking the error? One of the functions of peer review is administrative and technical review that allows the analyst opportunity to make the corrections before the data is released.

I performed my duties at or above standards. No cases were intentionally jeopardized by me. If the weight of a certain drug changed, then the City is responsible because it did not have property inventory and proper storage facilities that were temperature and humidity controlled.

How can the City of Columbia Police Department fairly hold me solely responsible for its gross ineptitude? I refuse to be the City of Columbia-Police Department's scapegoat, and I will fight (using the faith of God's given grace and mercy) using every ounce of my soul to reclaim my good name, **Brenda Gale Toomer-Frazier.**

Below is the SC statue that was referenced for the lawsuit against the City of Columbia that was submitted on November 3, 2014:

Commitment, Service and Betrayal

Title 42 – USC - 1981, The Public Health and Welfare

1981, Equal Rights Under the Law, (b), Make and Enforce Contracts,

For the purposes for this section, the term "make and enforce contracts" includes the making, performance, modifications, and termination of contracts, and the enjoyment of all benefits, privileges, terms and conditions of the contractual relationships. NOW COMES PLAINTIFF BRENDA TOOMER-FRAZIER, BY AND THROUGH THE UNDERSIGNED ATTORNEY, COMPLAINING OF THE ACTS OF DEFENDANT, ALLEGING, AND SAYING THE FOLLOWING:

GENERAL ALLEGATIONS

1. Plaintiff Brenda Toomer-Frazier (hereinafter "Toomer-Frazier" or "Plaintiff") is a resident of the County of Richland, State of South Carolina, now and at all times relevant to this lawsuit.

2. Plaintiff is African American. As such, Plaintiff is a

member of a protected class for purposes of 42 U.S.C. § 1981.

3. Defendant City of Columbia ("Defendant City") is a duly incorporated municipality within the State of South Carolina, and was the employer of Toomer-Frazier at all times relevant to this lawsuit.

4. Upon information and belief, Defendant City, at all times relevant to this complaint, employed more than 500 persons.

5. On or about December 27, 2011, Plaintiff started employment with the Defendant City as a forensic chemist.

6. Plaintiff was initially hired in December 2011 as a forensic drug chemist for the Columbia Police Department. Subsequently, like white forensic chemists in the past, she obtained her certification as a Class III police officer for the City of Columbia.

7. In March 2013, Defendant City, through its agent or employee, informed Plaintiff that she could no longer

Commitment, Service and Betrayal

serve as a Class III Police Officer.

8. Plaintiff worked as a forensic drug chemist for the Defendant City from December 27, 2011 to September 12, 2014.

9. On or about August 25, 2014, Plaintiff was given the option of either resigning from her position as a forensic chemist or face termination. Therefore, by letter dated August 25, 2014, Plaintiff tendered her resignation from the forensic drug chemist position with the Defendant City, effective September 12, 2014.

10. Plaintiff's decision to resign her position with Defendant City was based solely on the options presented to her by Chief W. Holbrook, and but for the threat of termination, Plaintiff would not have resigned her position as a forensic drug chemist.

11. At all times relevant to this lawsuit, Plaintiff was duly qualified to hold the position as forensic drug chemist for the Defendant City.

FIRST CLAIM FOR RELIEF
Violation of 42 U.S.C. § 1981
(Intentional Discrimination)

12. Paragraphs 1 through 11 are incorporated herein by reference.

13. In her capacity as a forensic drug chemist from December 27, 2011 to September 12, 2014, Plaintiff and Defendant City enjoyed an employee-at-will contract.

14. Despite her status as an employee-at-will, Plaintiff's contractual rights against intentional discrimination were protected by 42 U.S.C. § 1981 (sometimes referred to as "Section 1981"), at all times relevant to her employment. *See, e.g., Spriggs vs. Diamond Auto Glass, 242 F.3d 3179 (4th Cir. 2001).*

15. The relevant portions of Section 1981, as amended in 1991, provides as follows:

    (a)   **Statement of equal rights**

All persons within the jurisdiction of the United States shall have the same right in every State and Territory to make and enforce contracts, to sue, be parties, give evidence, and to the full and equal benefit of all laws and proceedings for the security of persons and property as is enjoyed by white citizens, and shall be subject to like punishment, pains, penalties, taxes, licenses, and exactions of every kind, and to no other.

(b) **"Make and enforce contracts" defined**

For purposes of this section, the term "make and enforce contracts" includes the making, performance, modification, and termination of contracts, and the enjoyment of all benefits, privileges, terms, and conditions of the contractual relationship.

(c) **Protection against impairment**

The rights protected by this section are protected against impairment by nongovernmental discrimination and impairment under color of State law.

16. Based upon the plain language of Section 1981, Plaintiff, as an African American, enjoyed the same right to make and enforce her oral contract of employment on the same term and condition as is enjoyed by white citizens.

17. Prior to Plaintiff being hired by Defendant City as a forensic drug chemist, it was the customs and policies of the Defendant City that the drug chemist would select his or her own peer review teams. Peer review teams are absolutely critical because no drugs analysis results can be released by the department unless it has been peered reviewed.

18. Prior to Plaintiff being hired, the Defendant City had

allowed all former white drug chemists and at that time to select their own peer review teams. Plaintiff requested the right to choose her own peer review team but was denied such right.

19. Defendant City, through its managers at the Columbia Police Department, chose Plaintiff's peer review team, which consisted of a drug chemist from Lexington County, State of South Carolina and other counties.

20. Without reason or cause, the drug chemist from Lexington County did not want to work with the Plaintiff initially.

21. The peer review team that was eventually established for Plaintiff was turbulent for the last 1 ½ years of Plaintiff employment with the Defendant City.

22. By failing to allow Plaintiff to select her own peer review team, Defendant City denied Plaintiff the right to make and enforce her oral contract of employment on the same terms and conditions as formerly situated white drug chemists, thereby, violating 42 U.S.C. § 1981.

23. Defendant City's act of selecting a peer review team for Plaintiff was intentional and purposeful discrimination against the Plaintiff, which was caused by a custom and unwritten policy of the Defendant City or such discriminatory decision was made by a person possessing a high enough rank to impute policy-making authority, all in violation of 42 U.S.C. § 1981.

24. Defendant City also intentionally and discriminatorily deprived Plaintiff of the necessary SLED-required training that it provided other similarly situated white drug chemists, in violation of 42 U.S.C. § 1981.

25. Further, Defendant City denied Plaintiff fringe benefits/"perks" that it normally provided to white drug chemists, to wit: removed Plaintiff from the status of a certified police officer; deprived Plaintiff of an automobile; altered Plaintiff's status in such a manner that removed the Plaintiff from the State's Police Retirement System; by refusing to staff Plaintiff's office with a sufficient number of drug chemists to meet the

work load, all which deprived the Plaintiff of the right to make and enforce her oral contract of employment on the same terms and conditions as white drug chemists, in violation of 42 U.S.C. § 1981.

26. All of the Defendant City's violations under Section 1981 were done in an intentional, discriminatory manner because of Plaintiff's race.

27. Defendant City's race discrimination concerned Plaintiff's "'making, performance, modification, and termination of contracts," or the fruits of her oral contractual relationship, and the said racial discrimination was caused by the policies and customs of the Defendant City or such discriminatory decisions were made by a person of sufficient rank to impute policy-making authority which allowed the Columbia Police Department to discriminate against the Plaintiff.

28. Defendant City had actual or constructive knowledge that it was discriminating against the Plaintiff by treating her different than similarly situated white drug chemists,

past or present.

29. As a direct and proximate result of Defendant's illegal discrimination in violation of 42 U.S.C. § 1981, Plaintiff suffered compensatory damages in the form, but not all inclusive, loss of employment opportunities, mental anguish, loss of sleep, humiliation, injury to her professional name, public ridicule, in an amount to be proved at trial but in no event less than $3 million dollars ($3,000,000.00).

SECOND CLAIM FOR RELIEF
Violation of 42 U.S.C. § 1981
(Retaliation)

30. Paragraphs 1 through 29 are incorporated herein by reference.

31. Upon information and believe, the Chief of the Columbia Police Department requested the Richland

County Sheriff Department, through Demetra ("Demi" Garvin) to conduct an evaluation of the drug analysis department. The evaluation is referred to as a "gap analysis".

32. Plaintiff was not given advance notice of the evaluation.

33. Demi Garvin (hereinafter referred to sometimes as "Garvin") appeared on July 11, 2014, without notice to the Plaintiff and commenced the evaluation of the drug analysis department.

34. At the commencement of the evaluation, Garvin urged Plaintiff to tell her everything because the evaluation could serve as a lightning rod to send help to the Plaintiff. Based upon the expectation that the evaluation would foster assistance from management in order to remedy some of the issues in her department, Plaintiff fully disclosed all of the issues to Garvin during the evaluation, including issues at that would put a reasonable person on notice that Plaintiff was not being treated fairly by not receiving the proper equipment or

training as similarly prior or present white drug chemists had received. Moreover, Plaintiff informed Garvin that the white drug chemist responsible for analyzing marijuana was not required to have his work peer reviewed, in violation of protocol, but the Plaintiff was required to have all work peer reviewed before releasing her results.

35. Based upon the manner in which Plaintiff complained to Garvin, Plaintiff's intra-organizational complaints were protected from the anti-retaliation mandates of 42 U.S.C. § 1981 as interpreted by binding case law,

36. as recognized by *Minor vs. Bostwick Laboratories, Inc., Case No. 10-1258, (4th Circuit, decided January 27, 2012)*.

37. Plaintiff's participation in the GAP Analysis/Evaluation as conducted by Garvin on July 11, 2014 was protected activity for the purpose of 42 U.S.C. § 1981.

38. During Garvin's evaluation, Plaintiff complained about issues that would put a reasonable person on notice that

discrimination was occurring and she informed Garvin of several incidences where the Columbia Police department was operating the drug lab in violation of protocols or were operating the drug lab in such a reckless manner that criminal defendants' constitutional rights were in jeopardy. For example, the July 11, 2014 report includes evidence that Plaintiff informed Garvin of the following, not all inclusive: (a) that the Columbia Police Department had failed to identify all individuals who possessed keys to the laboratory and who had access to the large bank vault (storage vault which stored the drug evidence on a short term basis)(this vault contained the powdered drugs). Garvin's report specifically stated the following after receiving this information from Plaintiff: "There is currently no inventory being performed on these drugs, so there is no way to ascertain when/if inappropriate amounts are being removed/diverted;" (b) that it was taking Plaintiff too long to receive supplies that were ordered; (c) that the City was not properly calibrating its equipment (scales that are used to measure the amount of drugs) in the drug lab; (d) that training was needed for the in-house staff for evidence and property room; (e) that the daily operation in the lab exceeded the work of one analyst. Garvin's report expressly stated the following: "The daily operations (case load) and quality and safety practices required in this laboratory extend beyond the capabilities of one analyst. . ." (f) that the white chemist who analyzed marijuana and trained by SLED was unsupervised but was previously answered to the prior white chemist but she was not allowed to supervise him.

39. As a direct and proximate result of Plaintiff's participation in the protected activity, by complaining to Garvin during the evaluation, Plaintiff was forced to resign on August 25, 2014, which is tantamount to forced termination.

40. Upon information and belief, none of Plaintiff's white supervisors were forced to resign or terminated, unlike

the matter involving Isa P. Greene, a black female who was forced to resign because of the actions or inactions of her subordinates.

41. But for Plaintiff's participation in the protected activity, she would not have been forced to resign on August 25, 2014. Therefore, there is a clear nexus between Plaintiff's participation in the protected activity and the adverse action of her termination.

42. Defendant City had actual or constructive knowledge that it was retaliating against the Plaintiff as a result of her participation in the protected activity.

43. Defendant City's acts of retaliation were intentional.

44. As a direct and proximate result of Defendant's illegal retaliation in violation of 42 U.S.C. § 1981, Plaintiff suffered compensatory damages in the form, but not all inclusive, loss of employment opportunities, mental anguish, loss of sleep, humiliation, injury to her professional name, public ridicule, in an amount to be proved at trial but in no event less than $3 million

dollars ($3,000,000.00).

THIRD CLAIM FOR RELIEF
Gross Negligence
(In Hiring Garvin)

45. Paragraphs 1 through 43 are incorporated herein by reference.

46. As Plaintiff's employer, Defendant owed Plaintiff a duty to exercise reasonable care in hiring an outside lab to conduct an evaluation of Plaintiff's department, when it knew or should have known that such evaluation would affect the terms and conditions of Plaintiff's employment.

47. Garvin was hired to conduct an evaluation of the drug lab.

48. In that Garvin's evaluation was being used solely for internal purposes, Garvin was contracted to perform a non-delegable duty of the Columbia Police Department.

49. The Defendant exercised sole control over Garvin as she performed the evaluation.

50. Defendant City breached the duty of care owned to the Plaintiff by selecting Garvin in a negligent manner.

51. Defendant breached the duty of care owed to Plaintiff in in one or more of the following particulars, not all inclusive: (a) by retaining Garvin's services when it knew or should have known that Garvin had a conflict of interest because she is the director of the Richland County Forensic Lab, which operates a for-profit public organization that competes for forensic consumers in the open market. By disclosing adverse results in the Columbia Police Department's lab, Garvin stood to gain because the closing of the lab would create monetary business for the Richland County Sheriff Department. Moreover, upon information and belief, Garvin operates a private forensic entity that works for the Richland County Sheriff Department, an entity known as Forensic Science Network, LLC with whom Garvin has a professional association. With said conflict of interest, it was impossible for Garvin to be objective; (b) by

selecting Garvin for the GAP analysis when it knew or should have known neither that Garvin nor the Richland County Sheriff Office was accredited to perform outside auditing by American Society of Crime Laboratory Directors/Laboratory Accreditation Board (ASCLD/LAB) or any other accrediting agency.

52. Defendant City breached the duty of care owed to the Plaintiff in a grossly negligent manner.

53. As a direct and proximate result of Defendant's gross negligence, Plaintiff suffered compensatory damages in the form, but not all inclusive, loss of employment opportunities, mental anguish, loss of sleep, humiliation, injury to her professional name, public ridicule, in an amount to be proved at trial but in no event less than $3 million dollars ($3,000,000.00).

FOURTH CLAIM FOR RELIEF
Gross Negligence
(Negligent supervision, training, and provision of equipment and resources)

54. Paragraphs 1 through 52 are incorporated herein by reference.

55. As Plaintiff's employer, Defendant owed Plaintiff a duty to exercise reasonable care in training the Plaintiff as a drug chemist.

56. As Plaintiff's employer, Defendant owed Plaintiff a duty to exercise reasonable care in providing the Plaintiff with the reasonable resources, including personnel and equipment, in order to assist Plaintiff in operating as forensic drug analysis lab.

57. Defendant breached the duty of care owed to Plaintiff in one or more of the following particulars, not all inclusive: (a) by failing to provide the Plaintiff the proper equipment and personnel in order for her to efficiently perform her assigned duties; (b) by failing to implement proper protocols to protect the drug samples from elements and thieves; (c) by failing to provide the Plaintiff the necessary training and professional development; (d) by failing to properly supervise the

Plaintiff.

58. Defendant City breached the duty of care owed to the Plaintiff in a grossly negligent manner.

59. As a direct and proximate result of Defendant's gross negligence, Plaintiff suffered compensatory damages in the form, but not all inclusive, loss of employment opportunities, mental anguish, loss of sleep, humiliation, injury to her professional name, public ridicule, in an amount to be proved at trial but in no event less than $3 million dollars ($3,000,000.00).

WHEREFORE, Plaintiff respectfully requests the Court to grant her the following relief:

a. Award Plaintiff a judgment for compensatory damages, for the damages alleged, in the amount to be proved at the trial of this matter, but in no event in an amount less than Three Million Dollars and no/100ths ($3,000,000.00);

b. Award Plaintiff the costs of this action, including the fees and costs of experts and other professionals, together with reasonable attorneys' fees;

c. Grant Plaintiff such other and further relief as this Court finds necessary and proper.

Plaintiffs demand a trial by jury on all issues of fact and damages in this action.

Glenn A. Walters, Attorney for Plaintiff

The next day after the press conference, I was making preparation for a doctor's appointment in Columbia, SC. Having many calls of unknown numbers on my home phone and cell phone, for the sake of sanity, I do not answer unknown numbers or return phone calls without a message from a sender... especially from persons that are not in my best interest. While getting dress for the doctor's appointment, my cell phone was ringing excessively from an unknown number that I made the wise decision not to answer. On the way while driving, this time the caller had made the decision to leave a message.

Once at the doctor's office, I had listen to the message. Unbelievable, it was from the previous chief who I was hired by in 2011 and left the department due to health concerns. Rumor had it that he left due to his involvement in a promotional and unethical scandal with several persons in the department and city government officials as well as infidelity with department personnel. In the message, he identified himself and had wanted a return phone call. Not wanting to speak or talk with him now, I had decided to return the phone call after leaving the doctor's office. Good thing the nurses did not check my blood pressure because I know that it had elevated out of normal range. I had gone from the white coat syndrome to make a choice to listen to one of the evil people from Sodom and Gomorrah (After leaving the police department, this how I had referred to this place).

Once in the car, I dialed the number and knowing that there was a good possibility that the call was being recorded. He picked up

Commitment, Service and Betrayal

after a few rings and had introduced who he was and why he was calling. He had wanted to offer his assistance with the lawsuit against the city's police department. Knowing that this was not a sincere offer, so I just continued listening to him rattle on about his experience after leaving the department. He had talked about how his cellphone would ring constantly but now… no one calls him from the department.

He now moved back to the country with his daughter in a house on a dirt road where he can monitor who comes on his property (meaning who comes to harm him). He had spoken of his initial meeting with the present chief of the police department and how rude the police chief was to him. At the meeting he had introduced himself and offer to assist the new police chief, but the new police chief had told him that I know who you are, and I do not need assistance from you.

Was I shocked with this information? Not in the least bit. Surprising and ironic, he offers help to me and the new police chief but not when I was working in the laboratory at the police

Commitment, Service and Betrayal

department. He never called and/or offered assistance at all. Once in the police department's elevator, he stepped in with me and said hello and never asked one question about the laboratory and how was I personally doing and then got off at the next floor. This was the only time that I had seen or talked with him before his abrupt departure.

Using intuition and a gut feeling, I know that he was also fishing for information. Referring to a spiritual lesson from my church pastor, he had taught the method of how to push the adversary (demonic spirits) away. Making the decision of talking about my spiritual growth of knowing who God is and how God is making it possible by giving me the strength to preserver through this storm. Deceitfully, he asked who the pastor is and where this church is located, and he may plan to attend. Knowing that this is just a ploy, I played along with his conversation until I had heard enough.

Next, I called my attorney, who stated that the ex-police chief called him as well with the similar story. My attorney stated that he rushed him off the phone because he, just like me, had known that this was just a ploy to circumvent the lawsuit against the city's police department. This also goes back to the original epiphany, THERE IS NO HONOR AMONG THIEVES AND WE, AS GOOD PEOPLE, SHOULD NEVER LOOK FOR SOMETHING THAT IS NOT THERE.

From the City of Columbia's prospective, I should have told them that I was discriminated against while performing the chemist's responsibilities. Over the past several years as well as throughout my career, this type of behavior had occurred and wanting to move forward without this type of career banishment (expulsion). Having an unrealistic thought, I was trying to overcome the racial discrimination obstacles to prove to the powers to be that I could excel under these conditions. Having to not make a formal complaint to the command staff and human resources, I did speak of these situations to African American colleagues throughout the years with the City of Columbia.

During the press conference, one of the reporters spoke of the tactic that was used as a method to hire African Americans under one set of standards and expectations and then change to another set of standards and expectations after hiring. Then stating that this new hire did not meet their expectations therefore they would eventually be fired, replaced and/or demoted. This method is called, "Bait and Switch."

A few weeks later, discovery and disposition stages of the lawsuit had begun. Not being overly astonished with the questions for the preparation phase by my attorney. These are the responses from the command staff, human resources, retired SLED chemist and City of Columbia's city attorney.

Police Chief Dispositional Comments:

I am aware that Ms. Toomer-Frazier has alleged that her race and complaints about race discrimination were the motivating factor in her separation from employment. I am also aware that Ms. Toomer-Frazier has alleged that she was denied training and improperly supervised. This is not true. My decision to close the drug lab was made before I was aware of Ms. Toomer-Frazier's race. During my service as Police Chief, I received no communication from Ms. Toomer-Frazier or anyone acting on her behalf regarding alleged racial discrimination occurred. I have full confidence in Major Oree and Deputy Chief Kelly concerning the training opportunities provided to Ms. Toomer-Frazier. I also have confidence in the analysis provided by Dr. Garvin and respect the concerns expressed by Solicitor Johnson.

Human Resources Manager Dispositional Comments:

I met Ms. Brenda Toomer-Frazier sometime after her employment in the position of Chemist in the CPD drug lab. Ms. Toomer-Frazier would occasionally speak with me concerning the other chemist, Melissa Hendricks. Based upon these conversations, it was my impression that there was a personality conflict between Ms. Toomer-Frazier and Ms. Hendricks. Ms. Toomer-Frazier also complained to me that her peer reviewers were friends to Ms. Hendricks. Like Ms. Toomer-Frazier, I am African-American. Ms. Toomer-Frazier never made any complaint to me about racial discrimination or indicated that her issues with Ms. Hendricks and peer reviewers were to her race. Additionally, I did not personally observe any indication of race discrimination directed toward Ms. Toomer-Frazier. I am informed that Ms. Toomer-Frazier has complained that she was removed from the Police Officer's Retirement System ("PORS") and lost access to a City vehicle when she decided not to pursue Class 3 Officer Certification. I had conversations with Ms. Toomer-Frazier about this decision. I encouraged Ms. Toomer-Frazier to maintain Class 3 certification in order to maintain some of her benefits. Ms. Toomer-Frazier responded that she did not want Class 3 certification.

Deputy Chief Dispositional Comments:

Following her selection as Chemist, I received a communication from then Captain, Oree, that Ms. Toomer-Frazier requested training through SLED. I communicated with SLED and informed Captain Oree that the requested training was not available. As an alternative to training to SLED headquarters, Captain Oree and I selected Professor Carlotta Stackhouse to provide training for Ms. Toomer-Frazier. Professor Stackhouse formerly served as a trainer at SLED, developed SLED training materials and currently serves as a professor at Morris College. During the course of Ms. Toomer-Frazier's employment, I received reports of conflicts between Ms. Toomer-Frazier and her peer reviews. I also became aware of a substantial backlog and errors in the operations of the drug lab. I never received any report from Ms. Toomer-Frazier or anyone on her behalf concerning race discrimination in her training or employment. I have no reason to believe that Ms. Toomer-Frazier's race played any role in the decision by SLED not to offer training. I have no reason to believe that Ms. Toomer-Frazier was treated differently during her employment with the CPD because of her race.

Retired Chemist Dispositional Comments:

From August 2004 through October 2009, I held the position of Assistant Director (Major) of the South Carolina Law Enforcement Division (SLED). In that capacity, I was responsible for programs within the Division of Criminal Justice Information Services. I have also been responsible for functions including drug analysis and toxicology. While employed with SLED, I provided training for drug lab analysts and created the training manual. I also served as a forensic chemist for approximately 15 years, responsible for cases assigned and testimony in local, state and federal courts. In 2012, the City of Columbia requested that I provide drug lab training to Ms. Brenda Toomer-Frazier. Because I have trained many of the chemists at SLED and we used the same course materials that SLED used at the time, the training provided to Ms. Toomer-Frazier was at least equal to that *provided through SLED. Ms. Toomer-Frazier's background was from the environmental side of chemistry that did not involve peer reviews, questions concerning procedures or require explanations regarding protocols. <u>It appeared to me that Ms. Toomer-Frazier did not fully understand the critical nature of the work of a forensic chemist and the need for documentation.</u> The frustrations Ms. Toomer-Frazier communicated to me regarding peer review appeared to arise from <u>legitimate questions by her peers</u>. Ms. Toomer-Frazier never indicated to me that she believed her reviewers were selected or performed their duties on the basis of race discrimination.*

City Attorney Dispositional Comments:

I have reviewed the gap analysis report of the Columbia Police Department Drug Analysis Laboratory conducted by Demi Garvin, dated July 11, 2014. I have also met with Chief Holbrook and other senior staff to discuss the findings and the operation of the laboratory. It has been determined that the *former drug chemist was involved with the testing of 746 drug cases. Of those 746 cases, 558 cases were peer reviewed consistent with the normal review process prior to disposition of the cases. The remaining 188 cases are currently pending disposition and are in the process of being peer reviewed. <u>It is my position that the peer reviews conducted in the 558 cases were sufficient to validate the findings in those cases. There has been nothing to suggest that the peer reviews did not follow the required guidelines and procedures.</u> The <u>current, on-going peer reviews of the remaining 188 should reveal the accuracy of the initial findings</u> and assist in determining the best course of action in those cases. I look forward to working with you to resolve the remaining cases awaiting disposition.*

From the above disposition, there were lies in all of them except the disposition from the city attorney who was not involved with the proceedings from the past two years and would present more technical savvy to determine the outcome of almost 600 cases. The approximate 600 cases were analyzed and meet the scientific protocol following SLED procedures that I used in the crime laboratory. These SLED procedures were dated from 2004. To my surprise, if the retired chemist from SLED, who had trained for CPD, should have had access to the updated procedures. She had stated in her deposition that she was employed at SLED from 2004 until 2009. While training for CPD and at the college's laboratory, she did not have a copy of the SLED procedures or should I say, she had not shown procedures to me.

Keeping It Moving Forward

For someone having an abundance of laboratory experiences, with very little support and obstruction from so many facets, I had the ability and fortitude to analyze 588 cases as well as the other 188 cases from September 2012 until June 2014 (21 months). This also included at least 3 to 4 months of training that occurred while away from the laboratory. The other 188 cases were analyzed during the time that I did not have a peer review team and the cases were analyzed due to directions from the Captain.

I was told to continue analyzing cases because they were going to put together a peer review team. Since leaving the laboratory, I was told that persons who would not identify themselves, were calling the solicitor's office and telling them to investigate the CPD crime lab. (Often wondering who these persons could have been).

Over the next several months, it would turn into a waiting

process to know of the State of South Carolina Court System (Richland County Judicial courts) response. It turned out to be as my attorney suspected it to be, in favor of the City of Columbia. Not being surprised of the outcome, my attorney made a request to meet to determine the next course of action. At this meeting, my husband and I were in total amazement of the conversation with our attorney.

Each time we would meet with my attorney, we discussed the current political atmosphere on the federal and state level in reference to its judicial impact on this lawsuit. Over the past couple of years, South Carolina legislators have been under the microscope for unethical violations on the usage of campaign funding. A first circuit solicitor was appointed to investigate and prosecute local government officials on their improper use of campaign funds for personal usages as well as acting as lobbyist without following regulatory guidelines.

On this particular afternoon, we were to meet with our attorney. He had expressed while he was away from the office, his paralegal called him and stated that a group of government officials were in the conference room and waiting on his arrival. My attorney arrived to find out that they were offering him the opportunity to run against this first circuit solicitor.

Their plan was for him to run against this solicitor with the hopes that he would win because this area is a predominantly African American community that elected its first African American mayor in the history of this county. He expressed that he told them to get out of his office because he realized that they were trying to replace him in order to have more control of the position that is held by the first circuit solicitor. He also receives calls from the mayor of the City of Columbia about other cases against them. Being in this role as solicitor… he will have to step away from all these cases as well as mine.

Over the past month, the first circuit solicitor removed several state legislators with the plans of removing several more from political office.

At this meeting, we discussed the next course of action of appealing my case with the South Carolina Court System to the Fourth Circuit Court of Appeals in Richmond, Virginia. Going into this lawsuit from the start, we (my husband and I) had plans to go to the Supreme Court... if necessary. If this is what it was going to take to clear my name and to get justification for the ill treatment that I had received from the City of Columbia... we were going to keep it moving forward.

In various other conversations with my attorney, if this were a Democratic political environment that is more liberal, my case will probably stand a better chance to be viewed based on the true interpretation of the law. In my opinion this is a Republican political environment that is more conservative and will view the law based on their interpretation to keep African Americans in the 1940 and 1950 eras.

Their view point is that this country had a chance to be transformed under President Obama's administration, so the African American population should be grateful because we are now better off than we were in the 1940 to 1960's.

As for this lawsuit, the City of Columbia would like to see you go away and to never be heard from again. The impact that I had on the drug analyses cases will last throughout the life of the

Commitment, Service and Betrayal

person who committed the crime. As long as the individuals are alive, I can be subpoenaed to testify in the cases because there is not a statute of limitation on the drug analyses. So, with that being said, the City of Columbia is intimidated and would want you to go away. This brings to mind, when I would see a person for the City of Columbia, their responses would be that I look really good. My questions would be, "What am I supposed to look like?" Often thinking of others who have been in the media for other situations, they had turned to alcohol, drugs and unfortunately to taking something that they cannot give back... their life.

Our judicial system is to promote and preserve peace, safety and dignity for all citizens. It should not be used as if they are playing a monopoly game with the person who holds the dice (power) to use it for their personal gain.

As noted by Leslie Calvin Brown,

> ***Other people's opinion of you does not have to become your reality. If you don't stand up for something, you may fall for anything. You have to know what is right for you and go after it regardless of what others say.***

Commitment, Service and Betrayal

For ALL that has been spoken and written about me by these people at the City of Columbia, Columbia Police Department, News Stations and Newspapers, they do not define who I am because none of these persons really know who I am. I have been the sacrificial lamb in their plan that did not achieve the results they had hoped for. Through this spiritual walk with God, I have learned to be careful when digging holes for persons, the twist is, you may be the one to fall in.

God has and always will be the final judge and jury, but I will continue the fight that God has given me. I have learned that the

people who really know me are those who really love ME. With the spirit of love from my family, in this life I have learned that, GIVING UP... IS NOT AN OPTION and IT IS ALL ABOUT HOPE, SO NEVER GIVE UP!!!

www.ingramcontent.com/pod-product-compliance
Lightning Source LLC
Chambersburg PA
CBHW020423010526
44118CB00010B/395